APQ LIBRARY OF
PHILOSOPHY

Edited by NICHOLAS RESCHER

LEIBNIZ
An Introduction to his Philosophy

NICHOLAS RESCHER

ROWMAN AND LITTLEFIELD
TOTOWA NEW JERSEY

© *American Philosophical Quarterly 1979*

First published in the United States, 1979 by
Rowman and Littlefield, Totowa, New Jersey

Library of Congress Cataloging in Publication Data
Rescher, Nicholas.
   Leibniz: an introduction to his philosophy.
   (APQ library of philosophy)
   Bibliography: p.
   Includes index.
   1. Leibniz, Gottfried Wilhelm, Freiherr von, 1646–1716. I. Series.
B2598.R45   193   78–11987
ISBN 0–847611–5

For
WILHELM TOTOK
whose extraordinary organizational talents and efforts
have put all students of Leibniz
into his debt

Printed in Great Britain

TABLE OF CONTENTS

ABBREVIATIONS

Throughout the book the following abbreviations of the titles of Leibnizian works are used:

DM = *Discourse on Metaphysics*

PNG = *Principles of Nature and of Grace*

Nouv. Ess. = *Nouveaux Essais (New Essays)*

Phil. = C. I. Gerhardt, *Die philosophischen Schriften* von G. W. Leibniz, 7 vols. Berlin: Weidmann, 1850–1863.

Math. = C. I. Gerhardt, *Leibnizens mathematische Schriften*, 7 vols. Berlin and Halle: Weidmann, 1850–1863.

Loemker = L. E. Loemker, *Leibniz: Philosophical Papers and Letters*, Amsterdam; D. Reidel, 1970.

PREFACE

This book offers a compact exposition of the philosophical system of G. W. Leibniz. It is based upon my earlier work on *The Philosophy of Leibniz* (Englewood Cliffs: Prentice Hall, 1967).

It is my hope that the book will serve its intended function—to offer a clear and reasonably comprehensive introduction to the extraordinarily rich realm of Leibniz' philosophy. So simple-sounding a task is not an easy one. Since Leibniz himself never *wrote* that systematic treatment of his philosophy that he clearly *conceived* for it, it becomes incumbent on his expositors to some extent to *construct* the system at issue in the course of endeavoring to *explain* it.

I am grateful to Cynthia Freeland for assisting with the revision, to Kathleen Reznik for preparing the typescript, and to Jay Garfield for helping me to see the book through the press.

Pittsburgh
February 1977

Chapter I

Leibniz' Life and Works

1. *Introduction*

The aim of this book is to give a systematic introduction to the philosophy of Leibniz—a synoptic picture that is historically faithful and substantively coherent and cogent. In providing this account, we seek to navigate in the narrow channel between the Scylla of uncritical exposition and the Charybdis of loose interpretation and hasty critique.

Leibniz' philosophy not only can, but must be viewed *as a system*, an intricate, unified structure which, like the rococo decorations of his time, was worked out with almost endless attention to detail. His prodigious intellectual labors and the quality of his philosophical workmanship polished this system into an unusually diversified yet coherent whole. The surface inconsistencies which later critics have reproved with such facility are generally found, on closer inspection, not to be there at all. An *internal* critique of Leibniz' philosophy on grounds of intrinsic incongruities and inconsistencies must consequently prove a relatively unrewarding venture. Insofar as Leibniz' philosophy is unacceptable—and this is something which cannot at this time be doubted—it is because of the unacceptability of its premises, and not because of gross inconsistencies in the way in which the system is worked out from its basic commitments.

No compact presentation of Leibniz can convey an adequate idea of the enormous diversity and richness of his philosophical writings. He never actually wrote one systematic treatise presenting his "system," but revealed it piece by piece in the course of innumerable articles, letters, and papers. This endows his philosophical exposition with a uniquely prismatic character, each of the major ideas being a leitmotiv that repeatedly comes to the fore from a great variety of perspectives. Like the world it portrays, Leibniz' philosophy is a unified whole that can be seen from innumerable points of view.

At the same time, the mass and diversity of his writings means that any exposition of his philosophy has to be a *reconstruction* of it, and must thus run the risk of error—particularly by ways of omissions and misleading emphases. This is a risk which any exposition must accept—there is, in the very nature of the case, no way of avoiding it.

2. *Leibniz' Life and Writings*

This chapter is divided into two separate parts. The first attempts to give a brief picture of Leibniz' life and writings, the second presents a summary overview of the Leibniz literature.

Gottfried Wilhelm von Leibniz was born on July 1, 1646, at Leipzig, where his father was professor of moral philosophy at the university. He attended school but loved working on his own and was largely self-taught from the German and Latin books of his father's library. Early in his teens he launched himself into an intensive study of logic, scholastic philosophy, and Protestant theology. At 15 he entered the University of Leipzig. During the first preparatory years, one semester of which he spent at Jena, he studied principally philosophy, natural philosophy, and mathematics. His baccalaureate dissertation of 1663 (*De principio individui*) was devoted to a subject—the principle of individuation—to which he was to give lifelong attention. The next three years were largely devoted to legal studies, and in 1666 Leibniz applied for the degree of doctor of law. As he was but 20 years of age, his application was rejected on the grounds of youth by the university of his native city, but was immediately granted at the University of Altdorf (near Nuremberg), where his highly original dissertation "On Difficult Problems in the Law" (*De casibus perplexis in jure*) secured him the offer of a university position. This he declined, his goal being to enter public rather than academic life.

Before reaching 21, Leibniz had not only earned his doctorate in law, but had published several original studies in logic and legal theory. The presence of such a prodigy in Nuremberg was brought to the attention of Baron Johann Christian von Boineburg (1622–1672), former prime minister to the elector of Mainz, and one of the most prominent political figures in Germany. Through his aid, Leibniz entered the service of the elector of Mainz in 1668, after some months in Frankfurt seeing a legal book through the press. Apart from official missions, all the rest of his life was spent in residence in various courts.

At Mainz he was set to work on writings of a political nature. The most important was a memorandum for Louis XIV suggesting that Holland, as a merchant power with extensive trade in the East, might be seriously injured through the conquest of Egypt (a scheme which would incidentally serve Germany's interests by diverting French expansionism from Europe). Nothing came of the project at the time, but the idea seems to have stayed alive in French official circles until it came to fruition in the time of Napoleon. In 1672, Leibniz was sent to Paris in the elector's service to promote the Egyptian scheme. Although the mission failed to realize its objective, it, and a trip Leibniz made to London in conjunction with it, proved crucially important for Leibniz' intellectual development, for he now came into direct contact with the wider world of European learning.

In 1672, when Leibniz was 26, Descartes' followers and disciples were in possession of the philosophical arena, and some who had personally known and corresponded with him were still alive [e.g., Thomas Hobbes (1588–1679)]. Leibniz was able to establish personal contact with such important Cartesian followers as Antoine Arnauld (1612–1694), Nicholas Malebranche (1636–1715), and Spinoza (1632–1677), whom Leibniz visited in the Netherlands in 1675. Spinoza and John Locke (1632–1704) were still young. Modern physical science was in its lusty infancy. Robert Boyle (1627–1691) still had many years before him. Isaac Newton (1642–1727), with whom Leibniz was to enter into a fateful correspondence, was only at the beginning of his career. The mathematician-physicist C. Huygens (1629–1695) became Leibniz' mentor and friend in the course of the Paris visit. The scientific firmament was replete with such luminaries as von Guerike, Mariotte, Papin, and Perrault in physics, van Leeuwenhoek in biology, and the Bernouillis, Sturm, Wallis, and Varignon in mathematics. Leibniz entered into contact and correspondence with virtually all of these scholars. (He came to collect correspondents on scientific topics as another man might collect rare books). The doors to this far-flung realm of European learning were first opened to Leibniz in the course of his Parisian mission.

In January, 1673, Leibniz traveled to London as attaché on a political mission for the elector of Mainz. There he became acquainted with H. Oldenburg, Secretary of the Royal Society, and other of its members. He exhibited to the Royal Society a calculating machine of his own devising, more versatile than the earlier machine of Pascal. In April, 1673, shortly after returning to Paris, Leibniz was elected a fellow of the Royal Society. In Paris he devoted himself intensively to higher mathematics, especially geometry, largely under the tutelage of Huygens, and at this point began a series of original studies that culminated in his invention of the differential and integral calculus.

While in Paris, Leibniz transferred from the service of the elector of Mainz to that of Duke John Frederick of Brunswick-Lüneburg. In 1676 he settled in Hanover at the Duke's request, traveling there via London and Amsterdam, where he held conversations with Spinoza, of whose (then unpublished) *Ethics* he was able to make notes.

For the 40 remaining years of his active life Leibniz continued—under three successive princes—in the service of the Brunswick family. He was on excellent terms with the duke John Frederick (d. 1679), and his son and successor Ernest August (d. 1698), but with the accession of George Louis—later George I of Great Britain—his position was much less favorable, and Leibniz eventually dropped from favor at court. In his hey-day Leibniz was for all practical purposes a minister-without-portfolio in charge of historico-legal, cultural, and scientific affairs. He managed the royal libraries and archives, conducted legal and historical researches, composed polemical tracts to justify various rights and claims of the dukes of Hanover, and he planned a reformation of the coinage and reorganized the mines. Though Leibniz lived in the atmosphere of petty politics in a small German principality, his interests and outlook were always wide-ranging and international.

From 1687 to 1690 Leibniz traveled extensively through Germany, Austria and Italy searching public records and archives to gather information for an official history of the house of Brunswick, and gathering materials for his extensive collections on European diplomatic and political history. After returning from Italy in 1690, Leibniz was made librarian of the ducal library at Wolfenbüttel by Duke Anton of Brunswick-Wolfenbüttel. He now organized material collected in his travels for a code of international law into two great books.

The electress Sophia, wife of Ernest August and heir-apparent to the British throne, as well as her daughter, Sophie Charlotte, who became queen of Prussia, were particular friends of Leibniz. Some of his philosophical writing, including the *Theodicée*, grew out of his discussions with these influential princesses. When Sophie Charlotte reigned in Berlin, Leibniz frequently visited there, but after her death in 1705 his visits to Berlin became increasingly rare.

After the accession of George Louis, Leibniz was pressed to concentrate his official efforts on his history of the house of

Brunswick (which at his death had gone no further than the period 768–1005). As the 17th century drew towards its close, he began to feel increasingly constricted. To one correspondent he wrote:

> But here [in Hanover] one hardly finds anyone to talk to, or rather one does not count as a good courtier in this country if one speaks of scientific matters. Without the Electress one would speak of them even less.[1]

But he now looked increasingly in other directions. He used his influence at the court of Berlin to promote the establishment there in 1700 of the royal academy (*Akademie der Wissenschaften*), of which he was elected president for life. Founding academies modeled on those of Paris and London was a favorite project with Leibniz. He urged upon Peter the Great the plan for an academy at St. Petersburg which was not carried out until after the czar's death. In the course of an official visit to Vienna from 1712–1714 he promoted (unsuccessfully) a plan for establishing an academy there. This Viennese visit did give Leibniz some satisfaction, however, for he received the honor of an imperial Privy Councillorship and ennoblement. However, these démarches in other directions caused annoyance at the Hanoverian court, where Leibniz came into increasing disfavor and his long absence in Vienna was much resented.

Upon the death of Queen Anne in August, 1714, Leibniz' master, the elector George Louis of Hanover, succeeded at the throne of England as King George I. Leibniz returned to Hanover in mid-September, but George had already departed for England. Leibniz was eager to follow him to London and play a greater role on a larger stage, but he was by now *persona non grata* with the king. Leibniz was instructed to remain at Hanover and finish his history of the house of Brunswick, working in the vacuum left by the general exodus of important courtiers. He died on November 14, 1716 aged 70, his last years made difficult by neglect, illness, and the distrust of the local public. (The Hanover clergy called him "*Lövenix*"—believer in nothing—and his reputation as an unbeliever made him locally unpopular.) Despite this, he retained to the end his capacity for hard work in pursuit of active researches in many fields of learning.

Leibniz possessed an astounding range of interests and capacities. Mathematics, physics, geology, philosophy, logic, philology, theology, history, jurisprudence, politics, and economics are all subjects to which he made original contributions of the first rank. The universality of the range of his abilities and achievements is without rival in modern times.

By prodigious energy, ability, and effort, Leibniz managed to be three persons in one—a scholar, a public servant and man of affairs, and a courtier—without letting any one suffer at the expense of the others. He possessed amazing powers for swift and sustained work, sometimes taking meals at his desk and spending days on end there, except for a few occasional hours of sleep. He was fond of travel and even while traveling in the rough conveyances of the day he worked at mathematical problems.

In contemporary accounts Leibniz is described as a man of moderate habits, quick in temper but easily appeased, very self-assured, and impatient of contradiction, his irascibility no doubt the result of chronic overwork. By all evidence he was a man of wise understanding in human affairs, wide-ranging in interests, charitable in judgment of others, and tolerant of differences in customs and opinions. Leibniz' interests imbued him with a thoroughly cosmopolitan point of view. In discussing resumption of the work of the French Academy after the Peace of Ryswick (1697) he wrote:

> Provided that something of consequence is achieved, I am indifferent whether this is done in Germany or in France, for I seek the good of mankind. I am neither a *phil-Hellene* not a *philo-Roman*, but a *phil-anthropos*.[2]

Leibniz was a man of middling height, pale complexion, and rather slender. Though he lived a rather sedantary life he was generally in good health—a sound sleeper with a good digestion and an even temper. He was a night-worker who did not like to rise early but generally worked late into the morning hours. While reading was a favored activity, he loved to mingle with people in society and hoped to learn something from everyone. He was somewhat irascible and did not suffer fools gladly. He doubtless felt (and was) overworked. His secretary said that he spoke well of everybody and made the best of everything. He is said to have been money-conscious and tightfisted. He was perhaps overanxious to secure the recognition and honour he believed due him for his work and services. But behind this lay an inseparable mixture of personal ambition and public-spirited desire to be in a position to advance the general good, which could only be done from a position of influence. Leibniz' services to the interests of learning was indefatigable and incredibly many-sided. In learning controversy in correspondence he was immensely patient and good tempered. He had a voracious appetite for knowledge of all sorts and his interests were literally boundless. (In his regard as in some others he was quite like his interesting contemporary, Samuel Pepys.)

A word must be said about Leibniz' philosophical development. Until he was 15 or 16, he was under the influence of the Scholastics whose works he read in his father's library. In the course of his studies of the sciences at the University he inclined to a materialistic atomism (of the sort to be found in Gassendi and Bacon), a position from which he was moved in the early 1670's by a complicated complex of anti-materialist influences. (Leibniz' thought was molded by a diversified multitude of thinkers whose influence will perhaps never be unraveled; among the ancients are the Platonic tradition and Plato himself; among the medievals, the scholastics as well as the "new" Aristotle; in the Renaissance, Nicholas of Cusa and the entire Platonic movement of the late Renaissance; among the moderns, the Atomists, Bacon, and Hobbes.) The rudiments of his monadism were conceived by 1675, but for the long interval 1675–1685 Leibniz devoted himself mainly to his official duties and to mathematics, logic, and physics. His ideas in metaphysics lay fallow, apart from his continued intensive assimilation of ideas—the influence on Leibniz of Hobbes and Descartes was now prominent, albeit largely by way of negation. However, it was as much the effect of his devotion to mathematics and physics as of any purely philosophical influences that turned him away from his early atomistic learnings. During the winter of 1685–1686 he returned to philosophy and, in a concentrated period of thought, worked out the details of his philosophical system and wrote several superficial sketches of it (primarily the *Discourse on Metaphysics*). As of 1686 Leibniz' philosophy had reached its mature completion, and all of his subsequent writing on the subject can be looked upon as exposing to public view further parts of an existing structure to which little or no substantial additions, in more than expository and ornamental detail, are being made.

The story of Leibniz' philosophical writings is complex. He published only one philosophical book, the *Essais de Théodicée* (1710), although he wrote a second, the *Nouveaux Essais sur l'Entendement Humain*, a critique of John Locke's *An Essay Concerning Human Understanding*, which he left unpublished upon Locke's death in 1704. The essence of Leibniz' mature philosophy was contained in a series of occasional articles he published between 1686 and 1716 in such journals as the *Acta Eruditorum* of Leipzig and the *Journal des Savants* of Paris. But behind these generally sketchy articles lay a vast series of essays and memoranda prepared for personal use and never put into form for publication. The format Leibniz selected for propagation of his ideas was letters to select correspondents. (It would seem he was less concerned about publishing his system for the world than securing the adhesion, or at any rate understanding, of a score or two of leading intellects.) It is from the personal memoranda and his vast correspondence that one is able to obtain a firm and balanced grasp upon his philosophical system: the published works are but a window through which one can glance into the various parts of a larger structure. *Qui me non nisi editis novit, non novit,*[3] Leibniz very properly wrote on one occasion.

3. *The Leibniz Literature*

As indicated by the preceding discussion, Leibniz was a compulsive writer. Letters, memoranda, drafts, and essays flowed from his pen in an endless stream, and only a small fraction of this mass of material was put into print during his lifetime. He could not bring himself to throw written material away, after his death his papers were collected in packing crates in the Royal Library of Hanover. This material is described in detail in

Eduard Bodemann, *Die Leibniz-Handschriften der königlichen öffentlichen Bibliothek zu Hannover.* Hannover: Hahn, 1895.
Eduard Bodemann, *Der Briefwechsel des Gottfried Wilhelm Leibniz in der königlichen öffentlichen Bibliothek zu Hannover.* Hannover: Hann, 1889.

Gradually, as generations of Leibniz scholars edited and published material, a more solid and rounded appreciation of the range and depth of his work became possible.

A complete bibliography of all of Leibniz' writings that had found their way into print until 1935 is

Emile Ravier, *Bibliographie des Oeuvres de Leibniz.* Paris: Felix Alcan, 1937. Reprinted Hildesheim: G. Olms, 1926.

A comprehensive survey of the secondary literature is given in:

Kurt Müller, *Leibniz-Bibliographie: Verzeichnis der Literatur über Leibniz.* Frankfurt: Klostermann, 1967.

In 1900 an agreement was reached between the Prussian and

French academies that a complete edition of Leibniz' writings should be undertaken. Four German and four French scholars were entrusted with the preliminary task of surveying the manuscripts in the royal library at Hanover. The joint project aborted during World War I, but after the war the Prussian Academy decided to proceed with a complete Leibniz edition (*Sämtliche Schriften und Briefe*) in six series: I. Historical and Political Correspondence, II. Philosophical Correspondence, III. Scientific Correspondence, IV. Historical and Political Writings, V. Scientific Writings, and VI. Philosophical Writings. A few volumes in several of these series appeared in the interwar period, but the project ground to a halt in Nazi times. (A few volumes prepared before the war were issued afterwards.) In the course of World War II the manuscript materials became scattered; most material that had been in Berlin for the Academy edition came into the possession of East Germany, and some of the Hanover material went to other libraries for safekeeping. Collaborative arrangements are now underway among scholarly institutions in East and West Germany for continuation of the Academy edition, and have resulted in the fortunate appearance of many volumes in recent years.

Until this elaborate project is advanced, the principal instrument with which the student of Leibniz' philosophy will have to work is

C.I. Gerhardt, *Die philosophischen Schriften von G. W. Leibniz*, 7 vols. Berlin: Weidmann, 1875–1890. (Cited as *Phil.*)

Other editions especially useful for particular subject-matter regions follow.

Leibniz' work in mathematics and physics:

C.I. Gerhardt, *Leibnizens mathematische Schriften*. 7 vols. Berlin and Halle: Weidmann, 1850–1863. (Cited as *Math.*)

Leibniz' historical and political writings:

Onno Klopp, *Die Werke von Leibniz ... Erste Reihe: Historischpolitische und staatswissenschaftliche Schriften*, 11 vols. Hanover; Klindworth, 1864–1884.

Leibniz' logic:

Louis Couturat, *Opuscules et gragments inédits de Leibniz*. Paris: Felix Alcan, 1903.

Leibniz' physical and technological writings:

Ernst Gerland, *Leibnizens nachgelassene Schriften physikalischen, mechanischen und technischen Inhalts*. Leipzig: B. G. Teubner, 1906.

Leibniz' ethics and theology:

Gaston Grua, *G. W. Leibniz: Textes inédits*, 2 vols. Paris: Presses Universitaires de France, 1948.
——, *Jurisprudence universelle et théodicée selon Leibniz*. Paris: Presses Universitaires de France, 1953.
——, *La justice human selon Leibniz*. Paris: Presses Universitaires de France, 1956.

Other editions of important Leibnizian texts include:

Yvon Belaval, *G. W. Leibniz: Confessio Philosophi* (Paris, 1970).
Ivan Jagodinsky, *Leibnitiana elementa philosophiae arcanae de summa rerum (Kazan, 1913)*.
Paul Schrecker, *G. W. Leibniz, Opuscules philosophiques choisis* (Paris: Vrin, 1966).

The principal English translation of Leibniz' philosophical work is

L.E. Loemker, *Leibniz: Philosophical Papers and Letters*, 2 vols. Chicago: University of Chicago Press, 1956. Second ed. in one volume, Amsterdam; D. Reidel, 1970. The Introduction of this work contains a useful bibliography of the Leibniz literature, more complete than the compact overview given here. (Cited as *Loemker* in the 1970 version.)

Other English translations of various Leibnizian works include:

H.G. Alexander, *The Leibniz-Clarke Correspondence*. Manchester: Manchester University Press, 1956.
J.M. Child, *The Early Mathematical Manuscripts of Leibniz* La Salle, Ill.: Open Court Publishing Co., 1920.
G.M. Duncan, *G. W. Leibniz: Works*, 2d ed. New Haven: Tuttle, Morehouse & Taylor Co., 1908.
E.M. Huggard, *G. W. Leibniz: Theodicy*. London: Routledge & Kegan Paul, 1952.
A.G. Langley, *New Essays Concerning Human Understanding by G. W. Leibniz*, 2d ed. La Salle, Ill.: Open Court Publishing Co., 1916. Has numerous notes and an excellent index. The appendices contain some of Leibniz' physical writings.
R. Latta, *Leibniz: The Monadology and Other Philosophical Writings*. London: Oxford University Press, 1898.
P. Lucas and L. Grint, *G. W. Leibniz: Discourse on Metaphysics*. Manchester: Manchester University Press, 1953.
H.T. Mason, *The Leibniz-Arnauld Correspondence*. Manchester: Manchester University Press, 1967.
Robert McRae, *Leibniz: Perception, Apperception, and Thought*. Toronto: University of Toronto Press, 1976.
G.R. Montgomery, *Leibniz: Discourse on Metaphysics and Correspondence with Arnauld*. La Salle, Ill.: Open Court Publishing Co., 1902. Revised by A.R. Chandler in 1924.

M. Morris, *The Philosophical Writings of G. W. Leibniz.* London: J.M. Dent & Sons, Ltd., 1934.

G.H.R. Parkinson, *Leibniz: Logical Papers.* Oxford: The Clarendon Press, 1966.

Patrick Reiley, *The Political Writings of Leibniz.* Cambridge: Cambridge University Press, 1972.

C.W. Russell, *G. W. Leibniz: A System of Theology.* London: James Burns, 1850.

Paul and Ann Martin Schrecker, *Leibniz The Monadology and Other Philosophical Essays.* New York: Bobbs-Merrill, 1965.

P.P. Wiener, *Leibniz: Selections.* New York: Charles Scribner's Sons, 1951.

The most important secondary works on Leibniz' philosophy are

Ernest Cassirer, *Leibniz' System.* Marburg an der Lahn: N.G. Elwert, 1902; photoreprinted, Hildesheim, 1962.

Louis Couturat, *La logique de Leibniz.* Paris: Felix Alcan, 1901.

Bertrand Russell, *A Critical Exposition of the Philosophy of Leibniz.* Cambridge: University of Cambridge Press, 1900. Second edition, London: George Allen & Unwin, Ltd., 1937.

Some other works on Leibniz available in English warrant listing:

W.H. Barker, *Leibniz in France: From Arnauld to Voltaire.* Oxford: The Clarendon Press, 1953.

C.D. Broad, *Leibniz: An Introduction.* Cambridge: Cambridge University Press, 1975.

H.W. Carr, *Leibniz.* London: Ernest Benn, Ltd., 1929; reprinted, New York: Dover Publications, 1960.

John Hosler, *Leibniz's Moral Philosophy.* London: 1975.

Hidé Ishiguro, *Leibniz's Philosophy of Logic and Language.* London: Duckworth and Company Ltd., 1972.

H.W.B. Joseph, *Lectures on the Philosophy of Leibniz.* Oxford: Clarendon Press, 1949.

Gottfried Martin, *Leibniz: Logic and Metaphysics,* Tr. K.J. Northcott and P.G. Lucas. Manchester: Manchester University Press, 1963.

G.H.R. Parkinson, *Logic and Reality in Leibniz' Metaphysics.* Oxford: Clarendon Press, 1965.

C.A. van Peursen, *Leibniz,* tr. by H. Hoskins. London: Faber and Faber Ltd., 1969.

R.L. Saw, *Leibniz.* London: Penguin Books, 1954.

A.T. Tymieniecka, *Leibniz' Cosmological Synthesis.* Assen: Van Gorcum, 1964.

R.M. Yost, Jr., *Leibniz and Philosophical Analysis.* Berkeley and Los Angeles: University of California Press, 1954.

Two useful recent anthologies of English-language papers on Leibniz are

Harry G. Frankfurt, *Leibniz: A Collection of Critical Essays*. New York: Doubleday-Anchor, 1972; reissued by Notre Dame University, 1976.

Ivor Leclerc, *The Philosophy of Leibniz and the Modern World*. Nashville: Vanderbilt University Press, 1973.

A work not specifically devoted to Leibniz, but nevertheless providing very useful background for the student of his philosophy, is

A.O. Lovejoy, *The Great Chain of Being*. Cambridge, Mass.: Harvard University Press, 1936.

The classic and most authoritative biography of Leibniz is

G.E. Guhrauer, *Gottfried Wilhelm Freiherr von Leibniz—Eine Biographie*, 2 vols. Breslau: F. Hirt, 1842.

A recent biographical compilation of great value is

Kurt Müller and Gisela Krönert, *Leben und Werk von G. W. Leibniz: Eine Chronik*. Frankfurt A.M.: Vittorio Klostermann, 1969.

The only biographies in English are two older works:

J.M. Mackie, *Life of G. W. Leibniz*. Boston: Gould, Kendall & Lincoln, 1845.

John Theodore Merz, *Leibniz*. Edinburgh and London: W. Blackwood & Sons, 1884.

Two works useful for setting the background against which the culture of Leibniz' place and time is to be understood are

P. Hazard, *The European Mind: 1680–1715*. Engl. tr., J. Lewis. London: Hollis & Carter, 1953.

R.W. Meyer, *Leibniz and the Seventeenth-Century Revolution*. Engl. tr., J.P. Stern. Chicago:: Henry Regnery Co., 1952.

In 1969, the journal *Studia Leibnitiana*, official organ of the International G.W. Leibniz Society, commenced publication in Hanover. Together with its periodic supplemental monographs (*Supplementa*) this publication has established itself as an indispensable tool for the serious student of Leibniz.

NOTES

1. *Phil.*, III, p. 175. Leibniz always stood on excellent terms with the electress Sophia, heir-apparent to the British throne.

2. *Phil.*, VII, p. 456. (Regarding references of this form see p. 9.)

3. "One who knows me only by the published works, does not know me at all."

Chapter II

God and Possibility

1. *God*

Leibniz, more than any other modern philosopher, took seriously the idea of a *creation* of the universe, giving it a centrally important place in his system. Like the theories of the medievals for whom he had such great respect, his system put God as the *author of creation* at the focal position in metaphysics.

God, for Leibniz, may be defined as "the perfect being."[1] His existence is not a seriously problematic issue; it follows directly from the idea (or essence) of his perfection, by reasonings along the lines of the Ontological Argument of Anselm as refurbished by Descartes, and also by other, related arguments—a topic to which we will return at some length. Indeed, all characteristics of God must inhere in and derive from His nature as "the perfect being." Three of these characteristics are of primary importance for Leibniz: omniscience, omnipotence, and (omni-)benevolence.[2] These divine attributes are the operative theoretical concepts in terms of which the drama of creation unfolds itself.

2. *Substance*

In the philosophy of Leibniz, as in that of Descartes and Spinoza, the conception of *substance*—a thing that has, or is capable of *being*—plays a fundamental role. Here "being" means "*unified* being"—Leibniz firmly espouses the medieval principle: *ens et unum convertuntur*. Leibniz defines a substance as "a being capable of action."[3] God, of course, is a substance—the primordial substance, the only substance that exists in its own right. All other substances are in the first instance mere possibilities whose actualization hinges upon God, upon the creation. The prime characteristics of Leibniz' *substance* are: (1) a substance is a simple, unified, perduring existence, simple not in the sense of logical simplicity, but in the absence of spatial parts; (2) a given individual substance is capable of functioning as the subject of propositions, the predicates of true propositions concerning the substance standing for attributes of the substance; and (3) substances are capable of uniting *inconsistent* attributes and are thus capable of change (i.e., having an attribute at one time but not at another), while always carrying, as imprinted on their own nature, the *principles* that govern the succession of their changes.

Against the Cartesian notion of physical substance as pure extension, Leibniz cast three objections of a fundamentally conceptual character: extension cannot comprise the essence of material substance because (1) it is an *incomplete* notion; (2) it is a *complex* and not a simple concept, since it can be analyzed further into plurality, continuity, and coexistence;[4] (3) the very conception of extension is in its genesis imaginary and phenomenal, since size, figure, and so on, are not distinct self-subsisting things, but are relative to our perception;[5] and above all (4) it lacks any basis for *dynamism*, for activity and action.

One can loosely describe Leibniz' individual substance as a spatio-temporal existent that is without spatial parts, but not without attributes, and with a perduring individuality. One of Leibniz' own characterizations, helpful but incomplete unless interpreted in the context of many variant characterizations, reads as follows:

> There are only *atoms of substance*, that is to say, real unities, that are absolutely devoid of parts, which are the sources of action and the absolute first principles of the composition of all things and, as it were, are the ultimate elements in the analysis of substantial things. One could call them *metaphysical points*. They have something vital, a kind of perception; and mathematical points are their *points of view*, from which they express the universe.[6]

In a cognate passage we read that the individual substances, the monads,

> cannot have shape, otherwise they would have parts. And consequently a monad, in intself, and at a given moment, cannot be distinguished from another except by its internal qualities and actions which cannot be otherwise than its *perceptions* (i.e., representations of the compound, or of what is outside, in the simple) and its appetitions (i.e., its tendencies to pass from one perception to another), which are the principles of change. ... It [viz. a monad] is as a center or a point where, simple though it is, an infinity of angles are found made by the lines that come together there.[7]

The identification of the simple (primitive) predicates entering into the defining notions of substances with the simple perfections of God is a point repeatedly insisted upon by Leibniz.[8] This aspect of substances draws together several strands of thought in Leibniz' system, such as his thesis of the varying degrees of their perfection (and correlatively their imperfection or finitude), and his penchant for the Ontological Argument for the existence of God. Moreover, it accounts for his conception of the immanence of God in monadic life, a view which led some writers to class Leibniz among the medieval and Renaissance mystics in whose ideas he displayed great interest.

3. *Substance* Sub Ratione Possibilitatis

Prior to the creation (and we think here not of literal and temporal but of figurative and conceptual priority) all substances aside from God existed, or rather *subsisted*—since *ex hypothesi* they did not exist—only as ideas in the mind of God:[9]

> in God is found not only the source of existence, but also that of essences, insofar as they are real. In other words, He is the ground of what is real in the possible. For the Understanding of God is the region of the eternal truths and of the ideas on which they depend; and without Him there would be nothing real in the possibilities of things, and not only would there be nothing in existence, but nothing would even be possible.[10]

It should be stressed, however, that although presence in God's thoughts gives to unexistent possibles whatever "existence" they possess, the *nature* of such possibilities is wholly self-determined and in no way subject to God's will. God only *houses* the possibilities (so to speak), he does not *make* them.

Since God is omniscient, His concept of the substance is not approximate and incomplete but descends to every detail of its (possible) career, and includes every single one of its properties. With respect to possibles, the principle obtains that alternative "descriptions" of the same thing must, unlike actual existents, be *logically* equivalent. In God's plan for ontological possibilities there is no room for the sort of incompleteness that figures in recipes for cooking or the plans of architects ("Take 1 pint of milk." But from which cow? "Use such-and-such a piece of lumber." But from which tree?). Thus every possible substance, not only the ones actually singled out for creation, is represented in the mind of God by what Leibniz calls its *complete individual notion (notio completa seu perfecta substantiae singularis)*, in which every detail of the substance at every stage of its (potential) career is fixed.[11]

For simplicity and convenience we may think of the complete individual notion of the (possible) substance as its *program*. The history of a substance is merely the continuous unfolding of its program with the same inexorable inevitability with which a mathematical series is generated in the successive development of its defining law. This lawfulness comprises the essence of the substance and is the source of its continuing self-identity: "That there is a certain persisting law which involves the future states of that which we conceive as the same—this itself is what I say constitutes the same substance."[12] In view of its specifications through its complete individual notion, every substance "contains in its nature a *law of the continuation of the series* of its own operations and [thus] of everything that has happened or will happen to it."[13] The complete individual notion of a substance is, of course, known only to God, not to mortals:

> The notion of myself, and of any other individual substance, is infinitely more extensive and more difficult to understand than is a generic concept like that of a sphere, which is only incomplete. ... Therefore, although it is easy to determine that the number of feet in the diameter is not involved in the concept of a sphere in general, it is not so easy to decide if the journey which I intend 'to make is involved in my notion; otherwise it would be as easy for us to become prophets as to be Geometers.[14]

The contemplation of substances—not as existent actualities but as subsistent possibilities—forms in God's mind a "realm of possibles" (*pays des possibles*) in which every conceivable substance is presented "under the aspect of possibility" (*sub ratione possibilitatis*).[15] In God's mind we find the entire gamut of cosmological possibilities. (Note here the echo of Nicholas of Cusa's idea of the world as *explicatio dei*, its history being the unfolding of the divine plan, the "reading off" in nature of the book of God.) This part of the contents of the divine mind, the possible worlds, presents an essential preliminary to a discussion of Leibniz' theory of creation.

4. *Possible Worlds*

Any actual state of affairs could, conceivably, have been different, for such an assumption involves no contradictory consequences. But if any actual state of affairs were different, then, since it is but the outcome of a natural course of development,[16] the entire universe would have to have a different history of development. In fact, we should have to resort to a world different from ours, involving another possible development of things: our hypothetical invetigation would lead us to another, altogether different possible world. Anterior to the existence of our world there was recorded in the divine mind entire infinities of notions of possible individual substances, whose only being at this point is that *sub ratione possibilitatis* in God's mind.

The all-embracing completeness of the very concept (i.e., the defining program) of a possible substance marks it as either compossible or incompossible with any other given substance, and the fact that a given substance is compossible with such and such others must be incorporated in its concept. Since each of these possible substances involves one possible history of the development of the universe, only those involving the same history are compatible with each other. Because the actualization of some possibilities is incompatible with that of others, the manifold of possible substances splits into mutually exclusive systems of "compossibles." God's choice of creation is not of selection among individual substances, but among entire possible worlds; His will thus being always general: "God never has a *particular will.*"[17]

By means of this principle the possible substances sort themselves out into *possible worlds*. The possible world of any substance is the totality of all substances compossible with it. Each possible world consists of a family of possible substances, every one of which is compossible with all the rest, and the individual characteristics (and therefore, as we shall see, the mutual relations) of which are determined in every conceivable respect by their individual defining concepts. This omnidetermination of all its descriptive aspects endows possible worlds with a very strong sort of informational completeness. No matter what proposition *p* can be articulated with respect to such a world, it will have to turn out that either *p* or else not-*p* (and exactly one of them) obtains.

The substances of each possible world are thus reciprocally adjusted to one another in a thoroughgoing, *total* way. To use one of Leibniz' favorite metaphors, the substances of a possible world "mirror" one another in their mutual accommodation.[18] Since the entire history of each possible world is determined in every possible detail in terms of the complete individual notions of its constituent substances, there is no question of God's direct, immediate intervention in the course of natural events. (The possibility of divine action *within* the course of history is denied by Leibniz, so he rejects on this score both occasionalism and the interventionalism of Newton's divine clock-readjustor. Leibniz does, in the *Theodicy*, admit the possibility of continuous "creation," but this is not a matter of the introduction of new substances but of the temporal *continuation* of existing ones in accordance with a pre-established program.[19])

5. *The Priority of Essence*

If the concept of creation is to be introduced into the ontological framework just outlined in a viable way, the question of the existence of a possible substance must not be pre-empted by its complete individual notion. Thus Leibniz must either (1) adopt (i.e., anticipate) the Kantian course of denying that existence is a predicate, or else, (2) granting that existence is a predicate, rule existence out from the sphere of predicates that can feasibly enter into the defining notion of individual substances. Although in view of the paucity of evidence one cannot speak very firmly, it does appear that Leibniz took the second course, being willing to regard existence as a predicate,[20] albeit one of a nondescriptive sort that cannot enter into the essence of a substance (other than God), being inevitably consequent upon the character of a *pre-specified* essence.[21] In general, *essence* has priority over *existence*.

The question can be raised: Is there anything to a Leibnizian substance over and above the attributes that belong to it by virtue of the predicates loaded into its complete individual notion? From the human standpoint the answer is *yes*—we actually do not ever know the complete individual notion of a substance, but encounter that substance only in experience (in fact, in confused perception). Even from God's standpoint an affirmative answer must be given, for an existing substance is, *ex hypothesi*, an existent, i.e., an entity or a thing, and its existence is never a matter of the attributes overtly guaranteed by its complete individual notion. While a substance is *specified* by the totality of the properties of its defining notion, it cannot be *identified* with this totality. It is the *thing*—the being or possible being—that *has* these properties, and not these properties themselves.[22]

6. *The Monads and God*

An existing substance that is a member of the actual, and thus of the best possible, world, Leibniz calls a *monad*. He did not introduce the term monad until relatively late in his career. In the *Discourse on Metaphysics* of 1685, the first systematic presentation of his doctrine, he spoke simply of "individual substances." He continued to use this term, sometimes alternating it with *substantial form* and *entelechy*, or (when appropriate in context) *soul* or *spirit*. The term monad first began to be generally used by Leibniz in 1696.[23] Little else can be said about this definition apart from considering a question that has created a flurry of controversy among Leibniz scholars: Is God Himself a monad?

The answer to this must be in the affirmative. God is a monad, but a very special and unique one, for he is the *supreme* and the *prime* monad. The idea that God is a monad was called into question by Bertrand Russell,[24] who proposed to regard as mere "slips" those passages where Leibniz explicitly speaks of God as one among the monads.[25] I think it unfortunate to charge an author with more mistakes than absolutely necessary, and see no reason why we must view Leibniz' declarations that God is a monad as errors from the standpoint of his system. That His status is fundamentally similar to that of the monads can be seen from the fact that He, like them, is an existing substance, indeed the supreme substance.[26] Leibniz explicitly assigns God a place in the scale of monads, holding Him to be the highest spirit.[27] Moreover, if God were not a monad it would be a contrastless qualification and senseless redundancy for Leibniz to speak, as he does often, of *created* substances and *created* monads, since God is the only noncreated existent in his ontology. In summary, we may regard it as certain that God has a place in Leibniz' system of monads, although this place is beyond any question a special and pre-eminent one.

NOTES

1. He is "*un estre absolument parfait.*" *Phil.*, IV, p. 427 (Loemker, p. 303).

2. This is explicit in, e.g., the essay *Causa Dei asserta per justitiam ejus cum caeteris ejus perfectionibus. Phil.*, VI, pp. 437 ff. Leibniz follows in the footsteps of the tradition of those who, like St. Thomas Aquinas, hold God to be perfect in being, knowledge, and wisdom. Cf. *Monadology*, §4.

3. "Principles of Nature and of Grace," §1. (This work is henceforth cited as PNG.)

4. *Phil.*, II, pp. 169–70 (Loemker, pp. 515–18).

5. *Discourse on Metaphysics*, §12. (This essay is henceforth cited as DM.)

6. *Phil.*, IV, pp. 482–3.

7. PNG, §2.

8. See, for example, *Phil.*, V, p. 15 (bottom).

9. To speak of anything "prior" to the existent universe is to use the term in a purely logical, and by no means temporal, sense; and when one does so, one deals with the necessary being, the necessary truths, and the possible worlds, i.e., one enters the sphere of pure logic. It is hardly possible to find here a place for activity of any sort.

10. *Monadology*, §43.

11. *Monadology*, §43. One state of a substance always summarizes all its others, so that "the present is always big with the future," as Leibniz puts it.

12. *Phil.*, II, p. 264 (Loemker, p. 535).

13. *Phil.*, II, p. 136; cf. DM §8, and Couturat, *Opuscules*, pp. 402–3, 520.

14. *Phil.*, II, p. 45.

15. This is the key idea of one of Leibniz' ways of establishing the existence of

God, since not even possibles would exist without the existence of "a being who could produce the possible" (*Phil.*, III, p. 572; Loemker, p. 661).

16. In Leibniz, one must remember, we are confronted with a strict mechanist.

17. *Théodicée*, §206.

18. It is derived from Nicholas of Cusa, according to whom the entire universe is a mirror of God.

19. Cf. DM, §xxx: "God in co-operating with our actions ordinarily does no more than to follow the laws He has established, which is to say that He continually preserves and produces our being in such a way that thoughts come to us spontaneously or freely in the order carried in the concept of our individual substance, in which it could have been forseen through all eternity."

20. *Phil.*, V, p. 339. Cf. Russell, *Critical Exposition*, pp. 77, 174, 185.

21. *Phil.*, VII, p. 195.

22. Jagodinsky, p. 95; Loemker, p. 160.

23. See A.G. Langley (tr.), *G. W. Leibniz: New Essays Concerning Human Understanding* (New York & London: Macmillan Co., 1896), p. 101, notes. Cf. also Gerhardt's observations in *Phil.*, IV, pp. 417–18. Prof. L.E. Loemker informs me, however, that Leibniz employed the term *monas* (pl. *monades*)—albeit in a mathematical sense—as early as the Leipzig period.

24. Russell, *Critical Exposition*, p. 187.

25. For example, *Phil.*, III, p. 636 (Loemker, p. 659); *Phil.*, VII, p. 502; Grua, *Textes inédits*, p. 393.

26. *Monadology*, §40.

27. *Phil.*, IV, p. 460 (Loemker, p. 326).

Chapter III

Three Fundamental Principles

1. *Subject-Predicate Logic*

Since the books of Russell and Couturat were published in the first decade of this century, it has become a commonplace that Leibniz is fundamentally committed to a subject-predicate logic. The orthodox subject-predicate logician is held to believe that every (meaningful) proposition is of the subject-predicate form, or—somewhat less stringently—that while such a proposition need not be exactly of this form, it must then be a complex proposition that can be obtained by combining strictly subject-predicate propositions with syncategorematic connectives. It must be said emphatically that Leibniz is not, strictly speaking, a subject-predicate logician in this sense of the term, for he does not hold the position in full generality—with respect to propositions of all logical types (including, for example, those about mathematical abstracta)—but *only with respect to propositions about substances*, i.e., about existents or possible existents.

Leibniz' version of the subject-predicate thesis is thus not a *logical* one regarding the general nature of propositions,[1] but a specifically *metaphysical* one about the nature of substances. It was bound up with his idea that a substance is defined as the thing it is through its complete individual notion and his belief that a true subject-predicate proposition must be such that "the content of the subject must include that of the predicate in such a way that if one understands perfectly the concept of the subject, one will know that the predicate appertains to it also."[2] The key point is that *all* truth about substances roots predicational theses about them, and does so in a way that becomes explicit through *analysis*.

2. *The Nature of "Analysis"*

The Leibnizian "analysis" of a proposition about a substance consists of two steps:

1. To scrutinize the list of properties of the substance that is the subject of the proposition in order to determine what is and what is not included in its complete individual notion.
2. To determine whether the properties imputed by the predicate of the

proposition to its subject are in fact included in this list (or is a derivative of properties so included).

If possession of the properties P and Q were included in the complete individual notion of substance #323, this fact would underwrite the analyticity of each of the following propositions:

"Substance #323 has the property P"
"Substance #323 has the property P-and-Q"
"Substance #323 has the property P-or-R"

It is important to recognize that Leibnizian "analysis" is a logical process of a very rudimentary sort, based on the inferential procedures of *definitional replacement* and *determination of predicational containment* through explicit use of logical processes of inference. This process is more complicated than Kant's mode of "analysis," which envisages only the presence of *explicit* predicational containments after definitional replacements have been carried out.

When more than a single substance is involved—perhaps in a relational proposition about two substances—the process is much the same, but on an extended scale. Thus the "analysis" of the proposition "Substance s_1 has the same color as substance s_2" would proceed as follows:

1. The complete individual notion of substance s_1 includes the color predicate C.
2. The complete individual notion of substance s_2 includes the color predicate C.
3. Whenever substance x has the color predicate X and substance y has the color predicate Y, and $X = Y$, then substance x has the same color as substance y.

Each of these is true "by definition," the first two with reference to the complete individual notions of particular substances, the third a general definition of the concept "has the same color as." On the basis of such definitions, the proposition in question can be derived by logical manipulations alone, using these definitions to eliminate defined terms. This procedure of definitional reduction characterizes the analysis of propositions. As this sketch (rightly) suggests, Leibniz agrees entirely with Hobbes' view that only definitions are primary truths.[3]

One further complication must be introduced. In the case of certain, especially complex, propositions, this process of analysis may be nonterminating (i.e., infinite). In the previous examples the analysis resulted in an explicit identity after a finite number of steps, but such a brief termination need not necessarily be the case, according to Leibniz. Analysis of certain propositions will not result in *explicit* identities; they are only *virtually* identical, in that their analysis comes closer and closer to yielding, but never actually yields, an actual identity. There can be no doubt that Leibniz' views on this, however greatly indebted to his work on the infinitesimal calculus, were influenced by the teaching of Nicholas of Cusa (in Chaps. i–ii of *De docta ignorantia*) that truly accurate reasoning about matters of fact would require an infinite number of inferential steps between the premises and the ultimately desired conclusion, so that the human intellect can only approach, but never attain, the ultimate precision of truth (*praecisio veritatis*).[4]

3. *The Principle of Sufficient Reason: Every True Proposition is Analytic*

On Leibniz' conception, the circumstance that definitively marks a proposition (of the subject-predicate form) as *true* is if that predicate is included in the list of characteristics comprising the definition—and, in the case of a substance, the complete individual notion—of the subject, i.e., that "the predicate is in the subject" (*praedicatium inest subjecto*). This conception of truth provides the basis for what Leibniz calls the *Principle of Sufficient Reason*, a principle basic to his entire philosophical system. Opposing the view that truth is a matter of arbitrary human conventions, as with Hobbes, or that truth is grounded in the arbitrary will of God, as with Descartes, Leibniz maintains that the truth and falsity of propositions invariably have a non-arbitrary grounding in "the nature of things." This is codified in his Principle of Sufficient Reason. According to the principle, *every true proposition is analytic*. As explained in the previous section, a proposition is analytic if a process of "analysis," substitutions for defined terms of their definitions, can reduce the proposition to an overt identity, a logical truth. The principle in question thus maintains that every true proposition is either finitely or infinitely analytic; its analysis either results in an explicit identity or the identity is only a virtual one that cannot be reached after any finite number of steps, but only "in the limit."

The analysis at issue here may, and generally will, be one which God alone can carry out, whereas we were mortals cannot. In one place Leibniz puts the matter as follows:

In contingent truths, however, though the predicate inheres in the subject, we can never demonstrate this, nor can the proposition ever be reduced to an equation or an identity, but the analysis proceeds to infinity, only God being able to see, not the end of the analysis indeed, since there is no end, but the nexus of terms, or the inclusion of the predicate in the subject, since he sees everything which is in the series.[5]

Unlike men, God can carry out this analysis because His processes of reasoning are not only of greater scope than ours, but also vastly more efficient: He can deal with concepts and truths *directly*, whereas for us such dealings must be indirect, through the mediation of words and sentences.[6]

4. *The Principle of Identity (or of Contradiction): Every Finitely Analytic Proposition is True, Indeed Necessarily True*

The converse of the Principle of Sufficient Reason would of course read *every finitely or infinitely analytic proposition is true*—a thesis which Leibniz also espouses. This can be broken up, however, into a pair of theses, to wit, *every finitely analytic proposition is true* and *every infinitely analytic proposition is true*. Postponing for the moment the issue of infinitely analytic propositions, let us focus upon the first of these principles, to the effect that all finitely analytic propositions represent truths. This thesis is Leibniz' *Principle of Contradiction*.

A finitely analytic proposition, it will be recalled, is one that is either explicitly identical ("An equilateral rectangle is a rectangle" is a favorite example) or else is one that can be reduced to an explicitly identical proposition by a *finite* number of steps of reasoning using definitions alone. Since this process of analysis is such as to exhibit that (and how) the predicate of the proposition is contained in the defining concept of its subject, it is clear that such a finitely analytic proposition will not only be true, but *necessarily* true. The *Principle of Identity* is thus the governing principle for the domain of necessary truths.

Such necessary truths, being analytic in character, are true *ex vi terminorum*. They are thus true under all conditions or circumstances—and in all possible worlds. When a proposition falls under the Principle of Identity, its denial would not only be false, but selfcontradictory, since it denies that the predicate belongs to the subject when the analysis in question shows that it does demonstrably so belong. Accordingly, the Principle of Identity can also be regarded from the negative angle as the Principle of Contradiction to the effect that the denials of (finitely) analytic truths are selfcontradictory. Leibniz frequently speaks of the matter in this way, and refers to the principle of the necessary truths—that all finitely analytic propositions are necessary truths—as the Principle of Contradiction. It is clear, however, that he envisages but a single principle, two alternative versions of which are at issue.

But it remains to consider the other—more problematic—half of the converse of the Principle of Sufficient Reason.

5. The Principle of Perfection (or of the Best): Every Infinitely Analytic Proposition Is True, i.e., Contingently True

When a proposition is not finitely but only infinitely analytic, its predicate cannot be shown to inhere in its subject by any finite process of demonstration—it is not an "actually identical" proposition, but is only "virtually identical," the identity being one that can be shown to obtain only "in the limit." But exactly how are we to conceive of such an infinite process of analysis that exhibits the "virtually identical" of an infintely analytic proposition?

Every possible substance is a member of some possible world, and its complete individual notion involves its entire history in the development of that possible universe.[7] To every state in the development of a possible substance there corresponds a state of every other possible substance of its possible world, a correspondence capable of varying degrees of closeness of agreement between its members. Thus within a possible world every substance "represents" every other substance more or less "distinctly," or, inversely, it "perceives" the other substance with a greater or lesser degree of "clarity" or "confusion." In this way, at each stage of its development every possible substance "perceives" or "mirrors" its entire universe, and moreover does so more or less clearly as the mean value of the degree of clarity of its perception of individual substances varies. One may call the degree of clarity with which at a given state a possible substance mirrors its universe its *amount of perfection for that state* seeing that such capture of multiplicity in unity is exactly what Leibnizian "perfection" involves. And what Leibniz terms the total amount of perfection of a possible substance is simple a measure of its amount of transitory perfection for *all* its states.[8] Consequently every possible universe also has an amount of perfection, the sum total of the amounts of perfection of the possible substances belong to it.

In His selection of one among the possible worlds for actualization, God subscribes to a certain determinative principle.

This is the *Principle of Perfection or of the Best*.[9] In accord with this principle God selects that universe for which the amount of perfection is a maximum.[10] This principle is a formulation of the thesis that, in His decision of creation, God acted in the best possible way. Accordingly a contingent proposition is true if what it claims actually exists in the world, and thus *if an (infinite) analysis shows that what it asserts is indeed a claim that characterizes the best possible arrangement of things.*

Since every substance has its own characteristic complete individual notion, all of its features are *necessarily* features of it—except for the issue of existence and its ramifications. Accordingly, *descriptive* propositions about a possible world (qua *possible* world) are never contingent. While possible worlds will indeed be infinitely complex, they never involve infinite complexities in the predicative sphere. Their infinite analyticity is, according to Leibniz, the crucial characteristic of contingent truth:

> The difference between *necessary* and *contingent truths* is indeed the same as that between commensurable and incommensurable numbers. For just as commensurable numbers can be resolved into common factors, so necessary truths can be demonstrated, that is, reduced to identical propositions. Moreover: in surd (irrational) ratios the resolution proceeds *in infinitum* and a common measure cannot be attained; yet a certain series is obtained, though it be endless. Analogously, contingent truths require an infinite analysis which can be performed only by God, so that he alone can know them *a priori* and with certainty. ... Hence, any truth which is not susceptible of analysis and cannot be demonstrated by reason, but receives its ultimate reason and certainty from the divine mind alone, is not a necessary truth. All the truths of this kind I call *truths of fact.* This is the root of contingency, and so far as I know, no one has hitherto explained it.[11]

The Principle of Perfection enables us to understand what Leibniz intends when he speaks of the contingent truths as analytic, but requiring an infinite process for their analysis. A proposition is contingently true if the state of affairs characterized by this inclusion involves a greater amount of perfection for the world than any other possible state; in sum, if the state of affairs asserted by the proposition is one appropriate to the best possible world.[12]

> All contingent propositions have sufficient reasons, or equivalently have a priori proofs which establish their certainty, and which show that the connection of subject and predicate of these propositions has its foundation in their nature. But it is not the case that contingent propositions have demonstrations of necessity, since their sufficient

reasons are based on the principle of contingence or existence, i.e., on what seems best among the equally possible alternatives. ...[13]

It is thus via the infinite comparison demanded by the Principle of Perfection that an infinite process is imported into the analysis of a truth dealing with contingent existence.

The Principle of Perfection is Leibniz' principle of contingence: it is in virtue of this principle that infinitely analytic propositions can be *truths.* Against the backgrounds of our exposition of Leibniz' conception of the infinite analyticity of the truths dealing with contingent existence, this should be clear. For it is due precisely to God's choice of the best of all possible worlds, and therefore to the Principle of Perfection, that those propositions dealing with the best possible universe deal with the actual one, and thus are true. It is indeed the Principle of Perfection which guarantees the truth of those propositions infinitely analytic in the sense discussed. Leibniz in one particularly revealing passage puts the matter as follows:

> But to say that God can only choose what is best, and to infer from thence that what He does not choose is impossible, this, I say, is a confounding of terms: 'tis blending power and will, metaphysical necessity and moral necessity, essences and existences. For what is [strictly or metaphysically] necessary is so by its essence, since its opposite implies a contradiction. But *a contingent which exists owes its existence to the principle of what is best (principe du meilleur), which is a sufficient reason for the existence of things.* And therefore I say that [morally necessitating] motives incline without necessitating [metaphysically]; and that there is a certainty and infallibility, but not an absolute necessity in contingent things.[14]

And it is clear from the very logic of the situation that the Principles of Sufficient Reason and of Contradiction require an additional principle of contingence. The Principle of Perfection serves this function: "A contingent existent owes its existence to the Principle of Perfection, which is the sufficient reason for existents."[15] Leibniz calls the "necessity" of contingent truths *moral necessity* as opposed to the *logical* or *geometric* or *absolute* or *metaphysical necessity* of necessary truths, and he states that "moral necessity stems from the choice of the best."[16] In §46 of the *Monadology* Leibniz speaks of "the contingent truths whose principle is that of suitability or of the choice of the best." And he systematically contrasts "the necessary truths whose necessity is brute and geometric" with "the truths whose source lies in suitability and final causes."[17]

6. *The Criterion of Goodness*

Suppose that God, contemplating a conceivable world *sub ratione possibilitatis*, finds it meritorious and chooses to *create* it, i.e., advance it from the status of a *possible* to that of an *actual* substance. Since He is omniscient, He knows the relationship of this substance to all the others that are compossible or incompossible with it. Being beneficent He wishes to *maximize existence*, to create as much as possible,[18] and thus would not choose to actualize a certain possible substance without actualizing other substances compossible with it—i.e., its entire possible world. But which of the possible worlds is God to choose for actualization? Clearly, the answer must be *the best*.[19] But what criterion of merit does God employ to determine whether one possible world is more or less perfect than another?

The standard of relative perfection must thus play the pivotal role in the drama of creation. Leibniz was bitterly opposed the position of Descartes and Spinoza, whom Leibniz took to maintain the indifference and arbitrariness of God's will. Leibniz again and again insisted that there is an independent standard of the perfection of things—a standard determined by considerations of objective necessity, which the preferences and decisions of the deity could alter no more than the sum of two plus two. Moreover, this standard is not to apply simply to the actual domain of the real world, but is operative throughout the modally variant sphere of the merely possible as well. Leibniz held that possibilities are objectively good or bad by a standing "*règle de bonté*" that operates altogether independently of the nature of existence and of the will of God. Indeed this standard of goodness is the basis for two crucial modal distinctions: (1) since God acts for the best in all of his actions, that of creation pre-eminently included, it serves to demarcate the actual from the possible, and (2) given God's goodness, it renders the sphere of the actual as *necessary*—not in the absolute or *metaphysical* sense of this term, but in its relative or *moral* sense. The standard of goodness is accordingly pivotal for the operation of modal distinctions in the system of Leibniz.

But what is this criterion which a God who seeks to actualize *the best* of possible worlds employs in identifying it? By what criterion of merits does God determine whether one possible world is more or less perfect than another? This standard, Leibniz maintains, is the combination of *variety* and *order*.

The criterion of goodness or "perfection" for possible worlds is set forth by Leibniz in the following terms:

God has chosen [to create] that world which is the most perfect, that is to say, which is at the same time the simplest in its hypotheses [i.e., its laws] and the richest in phenomena.[20]

The characteristic properties of each substance change from one juncture to another in accordance with its program. The properties of substance #1 at one juncture may be more or less in accordance with and thus reflected or mirrored in those of substance #2 at this juncture. Out of these mirroring relationships grow the regularities which represent the "hypotheses," the natural laws of the possible worlds. The "best," most perfect possible world is that which exhibits the greatest *variety of its contents* (richness of phenomena) consonant with the greatest *simplicity of its laws*.[21]

> The ways of God are those most simple and uniform ... [being] the most productive in relation to the *simplicity of ways and means*. It is as if one said that a certain house was the best that could have been constructed at a given cost. ... If the effect were assumed to be greater, but the process less simple, I think one might say, when all is said and done, that the effect itself would be less great, taking into account not only the final effect but also the mediate effect. For the wisest mind so acts, as far as is possible, that the *means* are also *ends* of a sort, i.e., are desirable not only on account of what they do, but on account of what they are.[22]

We may think of the possible worlds as positioned along a curve of the following sort:

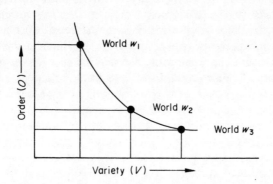

World w_1 is very orderly but lacks variety (it may, for example, be a vast sphere of copper suspended in air). World w_3 may be highly variegated—a virtually chaotic mixture of things—but lacking in order. World w_2 affors a much beter mix. Here the product $O \times V$ is as large as can be realized within the realm of possibility.

Accordingly the best of possible worlds is that which success-fully manages to achieve the greatest richness of phenomena (*richesse des effects* [DM, §5], *fecondité* [*Théodicee*, 208], *varietas formarum* [DM, §303] that can be combined with (*est en balance avec* [DM, §5], *sont les plus fécondes par rapport à* [*Théodicee*, §208]) the greatest simplicity of laws (*la simplicite des voyes* [DM, §5 and [*Théodicee*, §208], *le plus grand ordre* [PNG, §10]).

In the elegant essay *De rerum origionatione radicali* Leibniz puts the matter as follows:

> Hence it is most clearly understood that among the infinite combinations of possibles and possible series, that one actually exists by which the most of essence or of possibility is brought into existence. And indeed there is always in things a principle of determination which is based on consideration of maximum and minimum, such that the greatest effect is obtained with the least, so to speak, expenditure. And here the time, place, or in a word, the receptivity or capacity of the world may be considered as the expenditure or the ground upon which the world can be more easily built, whereas the varieties of forms correspond to the commodiousness of the edifice and the multiplicity and elegance of its chambers. (Loemker, p. 487.)

It is worthwhile to consider in some detail the individual components of Leibniz's two-factor criterion of variety and richness of phenomena on the one hand and lawfulness or order on the other.

The reference to lawfulness clearly carries back straightaway to Greek ideas (balance, harmony, proportion). The origination of cosmic order is a key theme in the Presocratics (e.g., Anaxi-mander) and becomes one of the great central issues of ancient philosophy with the writing of Plato's *Timaeus*. Afterwards, it of course plays a highly prominent role in the church fathers and achieves a central place in scholasticism in connection with the Cosmological Argument for the existence of God.

The prime factor in Leibniz' theory is not, however, lawfulness as such, but the simplicity or economy of laws. Leibniz, as we know, held that *every* possible world is lawful. As he puts it in §6 of the *Discourse on Metaphysics*: "we may say that in whatever manner God might have created the world, it would always have been regular and in a certain order." The critical difference between possible worlds in point of lawfulness is thus not whether there are laws or not —there *always* are—but whether these laws are relatively simple.

Regrettably, Leibniz nowhere treats in detail the range of issues involved in determining the relative simplicity of bodies of laws, and indeed he does not seem to be fully aware of the complexities that inhere in the concept of simplicity. Perhaps he did not think it necerssaey to go into details because it is, after all, God and not us imperfect humans by whom this determination is to be made. And in any case, it is clear enough in general terms what he had in mind. No one for whom the development of classical physics in its "Newtonian" formulation as a replacement of Ptolemaic epicycles and Copernican complexity was a living memory could fail to have some understanding of the issues. (It might be observed parenthetically that Leibniz would surely have viewed with approval and encouragement the efforts by Nelson Goodman, and others during the 1950's[23] to develop an exact analysis of the concept of simplicity operative in the context of scientific theories.) So much then for lawfulness; let us now turn to variety.

The situation as regards *variety* is even more subtle and complicated. As Leibniz considers it, variety has two principal aspects: fullness or completeness or comprehensiveness of content on the one hand, and diversity and richness and variation upon the other. All these factors are certainly found in ancient writers. They are notable in the *Timaeus*[24] and play a significant role in Plotinus and neoplatonism.[25] The church fathers also stressed the role of completeness and fullness (*fecunditas*) as a perfection, and it is prominent in St. Thomas's treatment of the cosmological argument and also in the later schoolmen. The recognition of the metaphysical importance of variety is thus an ancient and stable aspect of Platonic tradition.

But a new, Renaissance element is present in Leibniz's treatment of this theme: the aspect of *infinitude* that did not altogether appeal to the sense of tidiness of the more fastidious Greco-Roman mentality. The Renaissance evolution of a spatially infinite universe from the finite cosmos of Aristotle is a thoroughly familiar theme. And it represents a development that evoked strong reactions. One may recall Giordano Bruno's near-demonic delight with the break-up of the closed Aristotelian world into one opening into an infinite universe spread throughout endless spaces. Others were not delighted but appalled—as, e.g., Pascal was frightened by "the eternal silence of infinite spaces" of which he speaks so movingly in the *Pensées* (§§205–206). An analogous development occurred with respect to the strictly *qualitative* aspects of the universe. Enterprising and ardent spirits like Paracelsus, Helmont, and Bacon delighted in stressing a degree of complexity and diversity not envisaged in the ancient authorities. A vivid illustration of this welcoming of diversity is Leibniz's insistence that the variety of the world is not just a matter of the number of its substances, but of the infinite multiplicity of the forms or kinds they exemplify. He would not countenance a *vacuum formarum:* but taught that infinite gradations of kind connect any two natural species. Accordingly he was positively enthusiastic—as no classically fastidious thinker could have been—with the discovery by the early microscopists of a vast multitude of little squirming things in nature. Leibniz's concern for qualitative infinitude as an aspect of variety represents a distinctly modern variation of an ancient theme. In giving not only positive but even paramount value to variety, complexity, richness and comprehensiveness, Leibniz expresses, with characteristic genius, the Faustian outlook of modern European man.

There does, to be sure, remain the question of why it should be plausible to take this step and establish variety and order as conjoint but potentially conflicting yardsticks of perfection. The basis of plausibility of this Leibnizian standard rests upon a whole network of analogies, three of which are clearly primary:

> (1) *Art.* Throughout the fine arts an excellent production requires that a variety of effects be combined within a structural unity of workmanship. Think here of the paradigm of Baroque music and architecture, or again of the landscape gardening at Versailles or Herrenhausen.
> (2) *Statecraft.* Excellence can only be achieved in the political organization of affairs when variety (freedom) is duly combined with lawfulness (order and the rule of law).
> (3) *Science.* Any really adequate mechanism of scientific explanation must succeed in combining a wide variety of phenomena (the fall of an apple, the ebb and flow of the tides, the circumrotation of the moon, etc.) within the unifying range of a simple structure of laws (gravitation).

All of these diverse paradigms meet and run together in Leibniz' thinking. Like lesser luminaries such as Oswald Spengler and Ernst Cassirer, Leibniz had an extraordinarily keen eye for the perception of deep subsurface analogies. A true systematizer, he likes to exploit vast overarching connections and exhibits an extraordinary talent for transmitting a discernment of common structures into the formulation of a unifying theory.

His concern for an objective standard of cosmic valuation gives Leibniz a central place within the tradition of *evaluative metaphysics.* What he adds to the tradition is exactly to establish these two long-prominent *aspects* of the world's perfection as jointly operative and mutually conditioning criteria joined within a *single two-factor standard of the perfection* of a possible world. What is specifically characteristic of Leibniz is the idea of combination and balance of these factors in a state of mutual tension.

7. *More on the Principle of Perfection*

The existence of an objective criterion of goodness for possible worlds wholly independent of the will of God is a crucial feature of The Principle of Perfection. And Leibniz emphatically maintains that:

> In saying, therefore, that things are not good according to any standard of goodness, but simply by the will of God, it seems to me that one destroys, without realizing it, all the love of God and all His glory; for why praise Him for what he has done, if he would be equally praiseworthy in doing the contrary? ... This is why, accordingly, I find so strange those expressions of certain philosophers who say that the eternal truths of metaphysics and geometry, and so also the principles of goodness, of justice, and of perfection, are effects only of the will of God.[26]

The Principle of Perfection is Leibniz' philosophic formulation of the theological principle of God's goodness. It asserts that in the creation of the world God acted in the best way possible. The principle is not a logical, but a fundamentally ethical one, akin in its character to the jurists' dictum: *Quae contra bones mores sunt ea nec facere nos posse credendum est.*[27] Leibniz bitterly opposed the position of Descartes and Spinoza, whom he took to maintain the indifference and arbitrariness of God's will. He was eager to combat any manifestation of the view:

> ... the extremely dangerous [view], almost approaching that of recent innovators, whose opinion is that the beauty of the universe, and the goodness that we attribute to the works of God, are nothing more than the chimeras of men who conceive God after their own fashion ... [And who] also say that things are not good by any rule of goodness, but only by the will of God, one destroys, it seems to me, without realizing it, all love of God and all God's glory.[28]

That possible things are good objectively by a "règle de bonté" which is operative independently of the will of God, but that in His decisions of creation God freely subscribes to the valuation of this "règle de bonté" is the content of Leibniz' Principle of Perfection.

Leibniz repeatedly says that all possible substances have "a certain urge (*exigentia*) toward existence"; since to be a possible is

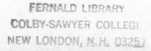

to be a possibly *existing* thing, we find in possibles a *conatus*, a dynamic striving toward existence proportionate to the perfection of the substance. This way of talking has led certain commentators, primarily A.O. Lovejoy,[29] to argue that Leibniz' talk of the selection of a (i.e., the best) possible world for actualization by God is a pointless redundancy, since it is the intrinsic nature of these substances to prevail in the struggle for existence among alternative possibilities. But this approach misconceives the issue badly, for it is only because God—in view of his *moral* perfection—*has chosen* to subscribe to a certain standard of *metaphysical* perfection in selecting a possible world for actualization that possible substances come to have (figurative) "claim" to existence. The relationship between "quantity of essence" or "perfection"[30] of substances on the one hand and on the other their claim or exigency to existence is *not* a logical linkage at all—a thesis which would reduce Leibniz' system into a Spinozistic necessitarianism—but a connection mediated by a free act of will on the part of God.

8. *A Polemical Digression*

The Principle of Perfection has been systematically misconceived by commentators. Couturat, for example, holds, as we have seen, that the pair of Principles constituted by Sufficient Reason and Contradiction is complete; consequently, he holds that the Principle of Perfection is subsidiary, and indeed a *consequence* of the Principle of Sufficient Reason.[31] Now this surely cannot be the case. The Principle of Sufficient Reason demands *definiteness;* it states that a contingent truth is susceptible of an analysis which, though infinite, *converges on something.* But such definiteness could have been gained equally well had God chosen the worst or the most mediocre of all possible worlds. The Principle of Sufficient Reason requires merely *that* a contingent truth be analytic; the Principle of Perfection shows *how* this is the case. As Leibniz repeatedly insists, the Principle of Sufficient Reason, being an a priori consequent of the nature of truth, leaves entirely open to God's choice a gamut of alternatives for possible creation, of which the best possible world is only one. Therefore, though it is true that the Principle of Sufficient Reason requires some complementary principle of definiteness, Leibniz would have been the first to deny that this *must* be the Principle of Perfection in the logical sense of "must." For this would at once lead back to the Spinozistic necessitarianism he is so eager to avoid.

Most commentators, including Erdmann, Latta, Joseph, and Russell, maintain that the Principle of Sufficient Reason is the principle of contingence, somehow subsuming the Principle of Perfection under this principle. Erdmann indeed goes so far as to identify the Principles of Sufficient Reason and Perfection.[32] This again cannot be so, not only for the reasons given, but also if we call to mind the previous characterization of Leibniz' three basic principles. All true propositions are analytic, finitely or infinitely (Principle of Sufficient Reason); all finitely analytic propositions are true (Principle of Contradiction); all infinitely analytic propositions—and thus all propositions whose infinite analysis converges on some characteristic of the best of all possible worlds—are true (Principle of Perfection). This is Leibniz' technical formulation of the three principles, and it puts their logical independence beyond doubt.

NOTES

1. To say this is not to deny that Leibniz thought the logical power of the subject-predicate form to be generally underrated. For example, he applied the subject-predicate formula not only to the four forms of categorical propositions, but to hypothetical propositions as well.

2. DM, §8.

3. Leibniz, however, departs from Hobbes with respect to the converse view that all definitions are truths, on the ground that definitions may involve contradictions, since "notions taken at random cannot always be reconciled among themselves" (*Phil.*, V, p. 425).

4. Nicholas even gives the mathematical analogue of the increasingly many-sided regular polygons inscribed in a circle whose content comes closer and closer to that of the circular disk in question without ever reaching it.

5. Loemker, p. 265.

6. These themes are pursued at some length in the *New Essays*; see especially Bk. III.

7. Leibniz claims that this is a logical consequence of the Principle of Sufficient Reason. The deduction he offers, along with a commentary, is given in Couturat's article, "La métaphysique de Leibniz" in *Revue de Métaphysique et de Morale*, vol. 10 (1902). See also the suggestive discussion by C.D. Broad, "Leibniz' Predicate-in-Notion Principle and Some of Its Alleged Consequences," *Theoria*, vol. 15 (1949), 54–70.

8. This theory of perception and its relation to perfection is presented in barest outline in Sections 14 and 49 of the *Monadology*. The following references prove especially illuminating as regards Leibniz' concept of perception: *Phil.*, I, pp. 383–4; VI, p. 604, p. 529. On the relation of perfection to perception see also *Phil.*, II, p. 451 (Loemker, pp. 604–5).

9. "Principle de la perfection," "*Lex melioris*," "Principe du meilleur," "Principe de la convenance."

10. This conception of the relation of perfection to existence makes it possible for Leibniz to identify the "quantity of essence" of a possible substance, which

determines its potentiality for existence, with its amount of perfection. "Everything possible ... tends with equal right towards existence according to its quantity of essence or reality, or to the degree of perfection which it involves, perfection being nothing but the quantity of essence" (*Phil.*, VII, p. 303; Loemker, p. 487). Since the more clearly a substance perceives another, the greater the compatibility of its own state with that perceived, perfection increases with compossibility. Thus, "just as possibility is the principle of essence, so perfection or the quantity of essence (which measures the number of compossibles of a thing) is the principle of existence" (*ibid.*). Hence the Principle of Perfection makes it possible for Leibniz to state that "one can define as existent that which is compatible with more things than anything incompatible with it" (Couturat, *Opuscules*, p. 360).

11. *Phil.* VII, p. 200.

12. We men, to be sure, do not see our way through the nature of things sufficiently to know *why* the particular developments of our world are for the best; we merely know on the "general principles" of the matter *that* they are.

> It is true that one may imagine [other] possible worlds ... but these same worlds again would be very inferior to ours in goodness. I cannot show you this in detail. For can I know and present infinities to you and compare them together? But you must judge with me *ab effectu*, since God has chosen this world as it is. (*Theodicée*, §10.)

13. DM, §130.

14. 5th letter to Clarke, §9 (italics supplied).

15. *Ibid.*, §9.

16. *Ibid.*, §76.

17. *Phil.*, III, p. 645.

18. Leibniz is fundamentally committed to the idea that existence is preferable to nonexistence.

19. We return to the topic of creation at greater length in Sec. 4 of Chap. 5.

20. DM, §6. Cf. *ibid.*, §5, and also PNG, §10; *Théodicee*, §208.

21. The *best* is thus *ipso facto* the most *harmonious* world, given that harmony for Leibniz "is, in effect, unity in multiplicity, it is greatest when it is the unity of the greatest number of apparently disorderly elements, which are resolved into ... the greatest concordance." (*Confessio Philosophi*, ed. and tr. by Y. Belaval [Paris, 1970], pp. 44–5.

22. *Théodicee*, §208.

23. Nelson Goodman, *The Structure of Appearance* (Cambridge, Mass., 1951; 2nd ed., Indianapolis, 1966); *idem.*, "Safety, Strength, Simplicity," *Philosophy of Science*, vol. 28 (1961), pp. 150–151; John G. Kemeny, "The Use of Simplicity in Induction," *The Philosophical Review*, vol. (1953), pp. 391–408.

24. *Timaeus* 33B; cf. F.M. Cornford's and T.L. Heath's comments *ad loc.*

25. Recall the stress on generative energy and creative power in the *Enneads* of Plotinus, and passages like "This earth of ours is full of varied life-forms and of immortal beings, to the very heavens it is crowded" (*Enn.* II, 8; McKenna).

26. DM, §2.

27. "The things that go against moral principles are also not to be thought possible actions for us" (*Phil.*, VII, p. 278).

28. DM, §2.

29. A.O. Lovejoy, *The Great Chain of Being* (Cambridge, Mass.: Harvard University Press, 1936), p. 179.

30. "Perfection is nothing but the quantity of essence" (*Phil.*, VII, p. 303; Loemker, p. 487. The entire context of this passage in the essay "On the Radical Origin of Things" (*De rerum origionatione radicali; Phil.*, VII, pp. 302–8; Loemker, pp. 486–91) is crucially relevant to the present discussion.

31. Couturat, *Logique*, p. 224.

32. J.E. Erdmann, *Grundriss der Geschichte der Philosophie* (Berlin: W. Hertz,

1896), Vol. II, 227; R. Latta, *Leibniz: The Monadology, and Other Philosophical Writings* (Oxford: Oxford University Press, 1898), p. 67; H.W.B. Joseph, *Lectures on the Philosophy of Leibniz* (Oxford: Clarendon Press, 1949), p. 114; B. Russell, *A Critical Exposition of the Philosophy of Leibniz*, 2d ed. (London: Allen & Unwin, 1937), p. 25.

Chapter IV

The Theory of Contingence

1. *The Role of Contingence*

The question of whether or not Leibniz' metaphysical system makes room for genuine contingence—avoiding a general collapse into a universal necessitarianism of the Spinozistic type—is a heated issue of debate among Leibniz scholars. There is no question that Leibniz *wished* to find a place for contingence; time and again he made claims to have done so, and pointed to the rejection of contingence in the system of Spinoza as a cardinal defect in his philosophy. But numerous commentators, Russell prominent among them, have held this desideratum to be improper for Leibniz, leading him into logical incompatibilities with key tenets of his system.

This question of contingence is a crucial issue for Leibniz' philosophy, for there is one group of occurrences in nature whose contingency is a life and death matter for his metaphysics: man's choices, decisions, and free actions. If contingence goes by the board in Leibniz' system, so does free will, thus sounding the deathknell to that project of reconciliation which was a central motive for Leibniz—the construction of a philosophic system he regarded as capable of meeting all the rational exigencies of the world-view of contemporary science on one hand and of Christian doctrine on the other.

Leibniz' explanation of how it comes about that contingent truths are analytic, the analysis being infinite, but convergent is one of the key features of his metaphysics. As we have seen, contingency, for Leibniz, is marked by the fact *that* an infinite process enters into the analysis of a contingent truth.[1] As regards the question of *how* this is the case, the answer, in briefest, is that an infinite comparison process is involved, one on whose basis it is exhibited that the truth at issue is one of the characteristics of a "best possible" arrangement of a world. Leibniz argues that in the analysis of any statement concerning the contingent which is an effort to account for it or some of its aspects, these infinitudes of relata represent conditions that must be taken into account.[2] Everything in the world is mutually involved with everything else. (The Hippocratean dictum *sympnoia panta*—"all things conspire together"—was a favorite with Leibniz.) Since the analysis of a contingent truth must proceed over an infinity of related contingents to show that the world it characterizes is the best possible (or otherwise), this can never be achieved fully by man, although it can become more and more complete. The mutual adjustments of things to one another in their common world is such that the analysis comparison of this substance with others leads to an infinite regress:

> All the more are contingent or infinite truths subject to the knowledge of God and known by him, not by demonstration—for this would involve contradiction—but by an infallible vision. ... [T]here can and must be truths which cannot be reduced by any analysis to identities or to the principle of contradiction but which involve an infinite series of reasons which only God can see through.[3]

2. The Principle of Perfection as a Maximization Principle

Since *true* contingent propositions concern contingent *existence* (with one important exception, as we shall see), the comparison of alternative existents enters into all of them. In this way the principle of contingent existence, the Principle of Perfection, enters into their analysis.[4] It is via this principle, and comparison of perfection of an infinite number of possible worlds involved in it, that an infinite process is imported into the analysis of contingent truths. The infinite analysis of a contingent truth is conceived of on an analogy with the infinitistic comparison problems of the calculus of variations. This branch of mathematics, which numbers Leibniz among its founders, handles problems such as selecting from among the infinite number of equiperimetric triangles that of maximum area or from among the infinite number of curves that of fastest descent. Correspondingly, under the auspices of the Principle of Perfection, the divine mind solves such problems as selecting that possible world with the maximum of perfection, or that possible Adam whose existence entails the greatest number of desirable consequences.[5]

Thus the Principle of Perfection provides the explanation of, and the mechanism for, the infinite analysis of contingent truths. A given proposition of the contingent type is true, and its subject includes its predicate, if the state of affairs characterized by this inclusion allows of greater perfection for the world than any other state of affairs. A truth of fact is such that the state of affairs it asserts is one belonging to the best of all possible worlds, hence its analysis, which consists in showing that this is indeed so, requires an infinite process of comparison.

In accord with the Principle of Perfection, the actual world as a whole is as perfect as possible and each of its parts is itself, in turn, as perfect as possible. There are not, as with Descartes, partial imperfections compensated for by the perfection of the whole. Each part of the world aids in the maximization of perfection by contributing the maximum of perfection that is, under the circumstances, possible for it.[6]

Thus the Principle of Perfection is a maximum principle, and it furnishes the mechanism of God's decision among the infinite, mutually exclusive systems of compossibles. It has as its immediate consequence that God actualized that possible world in which perfection is at a maximum. God is perfect, and consequently the only outlet for that perfection—the world—is perfect. Within the limits of possibility the actual world contains the most perfection, hence also the most existence.[7]

The Principle of Perfection resembles physical principles of a familiar kind. Leibniz himself makes much of such as the optical principles of least (or greatest, as the case may be) time and distance, and the principle of least action. The Principle of Perfection also specifies that in nature some quantity is at a maximum or a minimum, an idea which Leibniz often illustrates with the remark that in nature a drop of water will, if undisturbed, take on the form of a sphere, enclosing a maximal volume with a surface of given area. In other words, we have a "minimax" or "extremal" principle.[8] Like the others, it requires techniques analogous to those of the calculus, especially the calculus of variations. And the principle was in fact suggested to Leibniz by mathematical considerations. The background here is important for a proper understanding of his thought.

The remark is due to Hero, and is also to be found in the Ptolemaic corpus, that in traveling from one point to another via a plane mirror, a ray of light takes the shortest path.[9] In Leibniz' day a generalized version of this principle was beginning to find a place in optics. In about 1628 Fermat had developed a principle of least time which, together with a method of maxima and minima which anticipated the calculus, he used to deduce the laws of reflection and the newly discovered law of refraction.[10] Leibniz ardently espoused this principle, and reproached Descartes with having used, in accordance with the Cartesian program, a more clumsy mechanical method in the derivation of Snell's law of refraction, instead of the more elegant and fundamental principle of least time or distance.[11]

The mathematical problem of maxima and minima led Leibniz to extend Fermat's investigations, and resulted in invention of the differential calculus, but this does not concern us here. However, the optical minimum principle of least time also absorbed much of Leibniz' time and interest, and he generalized it in an important way.

This generalization of Fermat's principle of least time (or, equivalently in the case of a constant speed, of least distance) is to the effect that there need not be, in the usual transmission phenomena, a *minimization* of time. As Leibniz rightly points out, there might be a maximization, for example, in the case of a concave mirror.[12] But this does not undermine the general principle, for Leibniz remarks that the mathematical method for finding maxima and minima which he developed—finding a zero of the first derivative—yields both maxima and minima without discriminating between them.[13]

Inspired by its success in optics, Leibniz sought ardently to extend the applicability of minimax principles by means of a general principle that in all natural processes some physical quantity is at a maximum or a minimum. He felt he had found a principle which cuts across the particular laws of physics, and clearly demonstrates the general interconnection of things. Here was a powerful unifying rule for the multitude of particular natural laws, giving coherence to natural science and showing clearly the economy in nature. He could draw upon pure mathematics, mechanics, optics, and dynamics for illustration of his principle.[14] It makes possible the deduction of a multitude of particular laws from a simple general rule, and gives some insight into that remarkable unity of the phenomena on which Leibniz dwelt so fondly.[15] Let us consider just two of the examples which Leibniz regarded as illustrative of the unifying power revealed by this principle.

When one applies the rule of least time to obtain the law of refraction for a ray of light moving in the indicated direction from medium 1 to medium 2, with velocity $v(1)$ in medium 1 and $v(2)$ in medium 2, and with angle of incidence $A(1)$ and angle of refraction $A(2)$, one obtains the law: $v(1) : \sin A(1) :: v(2) : \sin A(2)$. But the law of reflection due to Hero (law of least distance, angle of incidence = angle of reflection, is merely a special case of this law, for in reflection the ray remains in the same medium, hence its velocity remains the same.[16]

Another instance of the "conspiration universelle" revealed in the application of the minimax principle is given by the solution to the Brachystochrone problem. This problem is to find a curve, the Brachystochrone, which has the following property:

> Suppose that two points in a vertical plane, A and B are given, A being the higher, and B located somewhere on the plane below. Let us imagine a particle starting from rest at A and rolling along a frictionless curved incline to B under the force of gravity (and a normal force exerted by the incline). The required curve is that one such that if the incline is installed along it the particle will accomplish its journey from A to B in the shortest time.[17]

It is necessary to determine "si ex datis pluribus infinitive quantitatibus invenienda sit una maxima vel minima," as John Bernouilli put it.[18] This curve of fastest descent, attainable by the mathematics of the calculus, is the cycloid, the curve generated by the motion of a point on the circumference of a wheel rolling along a straight line. This curve has another remarkable property: "If in the case of the curve of shortest descent between two given points, we choose any two points on this curve at will, the part of the line intercepted between them is also necessarily the line of shortest descent with regard to them."[19] This does not exhaust the interesting characteristics of this curve. If from any position on the curve a particle is released, and constrained to travel by frictionless rolling along the curve under the force of gravity (and the normal force exerted by contact with the curve), the particle will reach the bottom of the curve in the *same* amount of time regardless of the initial point selected (excepting the bottom point itself, of course). Thus the curve is also a tauto- or iso-chrone, a property which Huygens had already discovered by 1665.[20]

The noteworthy point is that in all problems of this sort belonging to the branch of mathematics now called the *calculus of variations*, the object is *to find one among an infinite number of alternative paths that achieves an extremization (minimization or maximization of some specified characteristic* (time, distance, and so on). What is at issue in such physical problems is an infinite comparison process leading to selection of an optimal alternative.

In his doctrine of contingence, perhaps more heavily than in any other part of his philosophy, Leibniz the philosopher is indebted to Leibniz the mathematician. The logic underlying this doctrine stems entirely and directly from Leibniz' mathematical investigations:

> There is something which had perplexed me for a long time—how it is possible for the predicate of a proposition to be contained in (*inesse*) the subject without making the proposition necessary. But the knowledge of Geometrical matters, and especially of infinitesimal analysis, lit the lamp for me, so that I came to see that notions too can be resolvable *in infinitum.*[21]

> At length some new and unexpected light appeared from a direction in which my hopes were smallest—from mathematical considerations regarding the nature of the infinite. In truth there are two labyrinths in the human mind, one concerning the composition of the continuum, the other concerning the nature of freedom. And both of these spring from exactly the same source—the infinite.[22]

3. *Contingentiae Radix*

We must now deal with a point which has troubled many commentators on Leibniz, and, regarded as perhaps the weakest spot in his defenses, has been one of the most prominent objects of attack by Leibniz' critics. The matter consists of a supposed conflict between God's freedom and perfection and the Principle of Sufficient Reason. It can be formulated in a dilemma. According to the Principle of Perfection, God acts in the most perfect way possible with regard to the creation of the world, and He does so either necessarily or freely. If He does so necessarily His freedom is destroyed, and all that follows as a result of His perfection—i.e., everything that happens in the world—is necessary. If He does so freely, in accord with Leibniz' principle, a sufficient reason must be adduced for this free act, and this in turn must be either free or necessitated. Thus an infinite regress is initiated.

Russell hangs Leibniz on the first horn of the dilemma.[23] He views Leibniz' system as *au fond* necessitarian, and regards the painfully drawn distinction between the necessary and contingent truths as null and void.[24] He charges Leibniz' system with involving that universal necessitation which its author was so ready to decry in Spinoza.

Although this problem is central to the philosophy of Leibniz, he never discusses it as fully and explicitly as one could desire. Still he did deal with, and to his own satisfaction solved, the problem of the reconciliation of God's freedom with the principle of sufficient reason.[25] This reconciliation, so necessary to Leibniz' system,[26] is to be regarded as one of its most original achievements.

As his 1671 letter to Magnus Wedderkopf shows, Leibniz'

earliest thinking came perilously close to an acceptance of necessitarianism:

> What, therefore, is the ultimate reason for the divine will? The divine intellect. ... What then is the reason for the divine intellect? The harmony of things. What the reason for the harmony of things? Nothing. For example, no reason can be given for the ratio of 2 to 4 being the same as that of 4 to 8, not even in the divine will. This depends on the essence itself, or the idea of things. For the essences of things are numbers, as it were, and contain the possibility of beings which God does not make as he does existence, since these possibilities or ideas of things coincide rather with God himself. Since God is the most perfect mind, however, it is impossible for him not to be affected by the most perfect harmony, and thus to be necessitated to do the best by the very ideality of things.
>
> This in no way detracts from freedom. For it is the highest freedom to be impelled to the best by a right reason. Whoever desires any other freedom is a fool. Hence it follows that whatever has happened, is happening, or will happen is best, and also necessary, but as I have said, with a necessity which takes nothing away from freedom because it takes nothing from the will and from the use of reason.[27]

As Leibniz penetrated further into the cross-currents of Cartesian philosophizing—as he entered more deeply into the thought of Malebranche and of Spinoza—he became increasingly discontent with a necessitarianism that blocked the way to genuine contingency in nature.

But nevertheless the major elements of his own doctrines all pointed in a necessitarian direction.

What alternative compossibility-systems there are is a *necessary* issue. Where they stand relative to each other in point of perfection is necessary. Hence that such-and-such a one is best is necessary. Gods creating the best is necessary. Hence existence of *this* world is necessary. Hence it is only seeming (only phenomenal *Schein*) that there are other possibilities.

Leibniz felt a deep dissatisfaction with this condition of things. As his oft-repeated criticisms of Descartes and Spinoza show, Leibniz was deeply committed to an authentic prospect of alternative possibilities. Leibniz emphatically did not want to have it happen—as did in fact happen among his interpreters as late as Russell—that he should be accused of Spinozism. This made him uncompromisingly determined *that* a place must be made for contingency, and all his relevant discussions indicate that Leibniz could not feel comfortable about promulgating his teaching until he had shown that his system provided a secure basis for avoiding universal necessitation.

That there be a valid for contingency.... But, *how—what*
place? This is an issue with which Leibniz grappled for a long, long
time.

And for good reason. The solution to the problem was not going
to be easy, seeming that most of the major doctrines pointed in a
necessitarian direction. But at last Leibniz saw a way out. A
combination of logical, mathematical and metaphysical ideas gave
him a way out of the labyrinth. The solution of the problem of
contingency within the framework of his other basic commitments—whose orientation is unquestionably necessitarian—was
difficult and represents one of the major intellectual *tours de force*
of Leibniz's philosophizing.

The starting point was his already well-entrenched idea that
there is a determinative principle to which God subscribes in His
selection of one among the possible worlds for actualization: the
Principle of Perfection or of the Best.[28] In accord with this
principle God selects that possible universe for which the amount
of perfection is a maximum. This principle indicates that in His
decision of creation God acted in the best possible way; so that the
actual world is the best among the possible worlds. But to yield
contingency, this ontological principle requires a logical sup-
plementation. We must consider more closely what Leibniz intends
when he speaks of the contingent truths as analytic, but requiring
an infinte process for their analysis. A given proposition concerning
a contingent existence is true, and its predicate is indeed contained
in its subject, if the state of affairs characterized by this inclusion
is such that it involves a greater amount of perfection for the world
than any other possible state; i.e., if the state of affairs asserted by
the proposition is one appropriate to the best possible world.

> All contingent propositions have sufficient reasons, or equivalently have
> *a priori* proofs which establish their certainty, and which show that the
> connection of subject and predicate of these propositions has its
> foundation in their nature. But it is not the case that contingent
> propositions have demonstrations of necessity, since their sufficient
> reasons are based on the principle of contingence or existence, i.e. on
> what seems best among the equally possible alternatives. ...[29]

An infinistic process is thus imported into the analysis of a truth
dealing with contingent existence. And this yields the crux of
Leibniz' solution of the problem of contingence, the idea that *the
analysis at issue with contingent truths ramifies through the
infinite comparison process demanded by the Principle of Perfection. Contingentiae radix est in infinitum* ("The ground of

contingence is in the infinte") is a cardinal maxim of Leibniz' philosophy.

NOTE

1. Leibniz, in criticizing Spinoza for failing to provide a definition of "contingence," wrote: "I use the term *contingent*, as do others, for that whose essence does not involve existence. In this sense, particular things are contingent according to Spinoza himself in prop. 24 [of Bk. I of the *Ethics*]" (*Phil.*, I, p. 148; Loemker, pp. 203–4).

2. "Indeed, even if the reason (cause) of a prior state could always be rendered from the one prior to that: yet its reason could in turn be given without reaching a last reason (cause) in the series. But this progression has the locus of its reason (cause) in the infinite, which, in some manner of its own, outside the series, in God, was immediately perceivable from the beginning by the Author of things, on whom depend both prior and posterior things, rather than [its being] he who, reciprocally, depends on them. Therefore whatever truth is not incapable of analysis and cannot be demonstrated from its own reasons but receives its ultimate reason and certitude only from the divine mind is not necessary. And such are all which I call *truths of fact*. And this is the root source of contingency ..." (*Phil.*, VII, p. 200).

3. Loemker, p. 266.

4. "All contingent propositions have sufficient reasons, or, equivalently, have a priori proofs which establish their certainty, and which show that the connection of subject and predicate of these propositions has its foundation in their nature. But it is not the case that contingent propositions have demonstrations of necessity, since their sufficient reasons are based on the principle of contingency or of the existence of things, i.e., on what is or seems the best among equally possible alternatives, while necessary truths are founded upon the principle of contradictions and [on that] of the possibility or impossibility of the essences themselves, without having regard in that respect on the free will of God or of creatures" (*Phil.*, IV, pp. 438–9; Loemker, p. 311).

5. "The true reason why this thing rather than that exists is to be subsumed under the free decrees of the divine will, of which the primary one is the decision to do everything in the best possible way, as seems wisest. Therefore it is occasionally permitted that a more perfect be excluded in favor of a less perfect; nevertheless in the sum that way of creating the world is chosen which involves more reality or perfection, and God works on the model of the master Geometer who in problems brings forth the best construction. Therefore all beings, insofar as they are involved in the first Being, have, above and beyond bare possibility, a propensity toward existing in proportion to their goodness, and they exist by the will of God unless they are incompatible with more perfect [existence-candidates:" (*Phil.*, Vii, pp. 309–10).

6. "The Principle of Perfection is not limited to the general but descends also to the particulars of things and phenomena and that in this respect it closely resembles the method of optimal forms, that is to say, of forms which provide a maximum or minimum, as the case may be—a method which I have introduced into geometry in addition to the ancient method of maximal and minimal quantities. For in these forms or figures the optimum is found not only in the whole but also in each part, and it would not even suffice in the whole without this. ..." And after citing as an example the remarkable properties of the cycloid, which we will later have occasion to consider, Leibniz continues: "It is in this way that the smallest parts of the universe are ruled in accordance with the order of greatest perfection ..." (*Phil.*, VII, pp. 272–3). But compare p. 142 below.

7. *De rerum origionatione radicali*, *Phil.*, VII, pp. 302 ff. (Loemker, pp. 486 ff.),

where: "existere quantum plurimum potest pro temporis locique capacitate." By "essence" Leibniz understands potentiality for existence, thus quantity of essence varies directly as perfection. "All possible things, or things expressing an essence or possible reality, tend toward existence with equal right in proportion to the quantity of essence or reality, or to the degree of perfection which they involve; for perfection is nothing but quantity of essence" (*Phil.*, VII, p. 303). Cf. *Monadology*, §41: "Perfection being nothing but the magnitude of positive reality taken in its strictest sense. ..." The actual world, therefore, having the maximum of perfection, contains the maximum of existence possible. Thus Leibniz gives the definition, "An *existent* is ... [that] which is compatible with more things than are incomptabile with it" (Couturat, *Opuscules*, p. 360).

8. See the *Tentamen Anagogicum* (*Phil.*, VII, pp. 270–9) on the minimax principles and their relation to the Principle of Perfection. The reader interested in the principle of least action in Leibniz is referred to the sixteenth note appended to Couturat's *Logique*, and to the Appendix to M. Gueroult's *Dynamique et métaphysique leibniziennes* (Paris: J. Vrin, 1934).

9. See E. Mach, *Science of Mechanics*, tr. P.E.B. Jourdain (La Salle, Ill.: Open Court Publishing Co., 1915), p. 518, and *Phil.*, VII, p. 274 (Loemker, p. 479). Hero flourished around A.D. 100 and Ptolemy around A.D. 130.

10. The law of refraction is due to Snell (1621). Cf. *Phil.*, VII, pp. 273–8 (Loemker, pp. 478–84).

11. *Phil.*, VII, p. 274 (Loemker, pp. 479–80).

12. *Ibid.*, pp. 274–5 (Loemker, pp. 480–1).

13. *Ibid.*, p. 275 (Loemker, p. 481).

14. See *passim* in the *Tentamen Anagogicum*, Phil., VII, pp. 270–9 (Loemker, pp. 477–84).

15. He termed it "la conspiration universelle."

16. See the *Randbemerkung, Phil.*, VII, p. 277 (Loemker, p. 483); and see Mach, *op. cit.*, p. 521.

17.

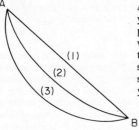

At first glance it might seem that a straight line, (1), yields the required curve. But it is clear that the particle would gain a greater velocity if it started with somewhat of a drop, as in (2), and thus more than compensate for the longer path by its greater speed. On the other hand if the initial drop were too steep, as in (3), the advantage of gained speed would yield to the disadvantage of added distance.

18. *Math.*, III, p. 303. Cf. n. 10 of the section on the principle of perfection. Moritz Cantor is imprecise in stating (*G. de Math.*, III, p. 225), that the name "Brachystochrone" for this curve first occurs in John Bernouilli's solution of the problem in the *Acta Eruditorum* of May 1697. Bernouilli had used the term earlier in a letter communicating his own solution to Leibniz which is dated July 1696 (*Math.*, III, pp. 295 ff.) from which we learn that the curve was almost destined to get another name. Here he writes: "I had given the line the name of 'Brachystochrone' for the reason you see here, but if the name 'Tachystoptote' is more pleasing, I permit that it be used anywhere in the place of the former."

19. *Phil.*, VII, p. 272 (Loemker, p. 478).

20. See Moritz Cantor, *Vorlesungen über Geschichte der Mathematik*, III (Leipzig: B.G. Teuber, 1880–1898), pp. 133–4.

21. Couturat, *Opuscules*, p. 18. Compare the important essay "On Freedom" in Loemker, pp. 263–6.

22. Couturat, *Logique*, p. 210, notes.

23. Bertrand Russell, *Critical Exposition*, p. 39, n. 1; cf. his paper in *Mind*, vol. 12 (1903), pp. 177–201, especially p. 185, n. 2.

24. Falsely, since this distinction is drawn on logical grounds alone.

25. See the opuscule *De Contingentia* (Grua, *Textes*, I, pp. 302–8).

26. This is so since God's freedom is one of the central tenets of Leibniz' philosophy. "God is always infallibly led to the best although He is not led necessarily (other than by a moral necessity) ... , it was not necessary or essential that God should create [a world], nor that God should create this world in particular, although His wisdom and goodness led Him to it" [*Phil.*, III, p. 402; letter to Coste (1707)]. Thus in Objection 8 of the *Abrégé en forme* of the *Théodicée* Leibniz criticizes the argument:

"Whoever cannot fail to choose the best, is not free.

God cannot fail to choose the best.

Hence, God is not free,"

Leibniz answers: "I deny the major premise of this argument" (*Phil.*, VI, pp. 385–6).

27. Loemker, p. 146.

28. "*Principe de la perfection*," "*Lex melioris*," "*Principe du Meilleur*," "*Principe de la convenance*."

29. *Phil.*, IV, pp. 438–9 (Loemker, p. 311).

Chapter V

Possible Worlds

1. *The Proliferation of Possibility*

A "possible substance" for Leibniz is not a shadowy sort of thing, a peculiarly insubstantial *kind* of individual, but the correlate of an *individual notion (or concept)*. A substance is a *concretum* that stands correlative to an *abstractum* of a certain sort—namely to a *description*. On Leibniz' approach, the ontology of possible individuals thus does not involve any mechanisms additional to the abstracta (attributes and concepts) that are in any case a basic mechanism of his metaphysics. Since possible substances are approached via this conceptual approach, there is a straightforward one-to-one correlation between *individual concepts* and *individual substances*.

The existing (real) world is a manifold of possible substances.[1] It is not the only such manifold—there are infinitely many others, each of which constitutes a possible world alternative to this one. Every possible world has its own population of possible substances. And not just *possible* ones, but substances that are also *compossible*, i.e., capable of being realized together and conjointly.

Every possible world is a *maximal* manifold of such compossible substances. There is never any addable possible substance—one that is not already a member of a given possible world and yet is compossible with the substances of this world.

2. *Tout est lié*

Every substance of every possible world has its characterizing complete individual notion that links it to all other substances of its world.[2] In consequence there is a (conceptual) linkage between the things of each world that render them indissolubly interconnected:

> In every possible world everything is linked together (*tout est lié*). The universe—however it might be constituted—is a unified whole, like an ocean; even the smallest motion extends its influence to any distance, however large.[3]

In consequence of these conceptual interconnections of a substance with all the others of its world, a substance stands to these others in a rigidly unalterable correlation. To change it (however slightly) in any way—even in thought—is to alter all the others as well—to "change the subject" as it were, by bringing into consideration an entirely different framework of things.

We thus arrive at a "one-substance, one-world" doctrine: every substance has imprinted on its defining nature (its complete individual notion) an ineradicable index of its entire environing world. No substance can—even in hypothesis—be pried loose from its world-environment and transposed into some other possible world. No possible substance can populate two distinct possible worlds, and no member of one world can be compatibly united with any member of any other.

3. The Identity of Indiscernibles

The preceding stance indicates that the substances of distinct worlds cannot be descriptively identical (indiscernible)—that substances in different worlds cannot possibly answer to the same complete individual notion. The principle now to be at issue extends beyond this. It stipulates that distinct substances of any one particular possible world cannot be descriptively identical with one another either.

This principle—the Principle of the Identity of Indiscernibles—was formulated by Leibniz in many different ways in different contexts. Some examples are: "No two substances are completely similar, or differ solely in number."[4] "There are not in nature two indiscernible real absolute beings."[5] In some of these formulations it might appear as though the principle applied only to the substances of *this*, i.e., the real, world, and failed to hold for other possible worlds. This impression would be mistaken, because this logically grounded, metaphysically necessary principle holds good within every possible world. In its logical formulation, the principle reads, apart from a confusion of use and mention, exactly like a rule of substitution for identicals in modern systems of logic: *Eadem sunt quorum unum in alterius locum substituti potest, salva veritate* ["Things are the same (or *identical*) one of which can be substituted in place of the other with preservation of truth"].[6] There can be no doubt that Leibniz did have in mind such a logical principle, analytically explicative of the very concept of identity, and thus valid for all possible worlds.

The logical rationale of the situation thus might be summarized by observing that the purely logical or conceptual dictum "one concept—one substance" furnishes the grounding of Leibniz' Principle of the Identity of Indiscernibles. A substance (i.e., possible substance) is—and must be—individuated through its complete description, its individual notion. Where there is only one such notion there is only one possible substance, since that individual concept is *its* concept. As Leibniz puts it in one passage: "To suppose two indiscernible things is to think of one and the same thing under two names."[7] A substance, prior to its actualization, subsists as a conceptual possibility in the mind of God. To arrive at another substance we would have to contemplate a change in the concept, altering the description at issue. Since the substances realized are chosen from among those whose defining concepts (complete individual notions) are entertained by God *sub ratione possibilitatis*, and since a substance so considered can only be considered in terms of its predicates (there being nothing else to individuate an individual concept), it transpires that distinct substances must in at least some respect differ in their properties, and thus have distinct predicates.

Leibniz did not hesitate to put a metaphysical construction upon this logical principle: If, of two possible things, #1 could be put in place of thing #2 in such a way that the descriptive structure of the world is left wholly intact—the truth of every proposition about it being unaffected—then things #1 and #2 are not two things but must be one and the same thing identified by different labels. But the foundation for this metaphysical thesis is purely logical.

Leibniz maintains the Principle of the Identity of Indiscernibles to be derivative from the Principle of Sufficient Reason. He explicitly considers this assumption that "two things perfectly indiscernible from each other did exist," and insists that "that supposition is false, and contrary to the grand principle of reason."[8] The reasoning here is readily understood: If there were two distinct indiscernibles *a* and *b*, then there would have to be present within the complete individual notion of substance *a* a truth regarding it—namely, that there are several other substances answering exactly to its own description—which could not reasonably be held to be something programmed into the concept of *a*, since *b* is conceptually indistinguishable from *a*. The principle should thus be regarded as grounded in the Principle of Identity, in view of the fact that it is conceptually explicative of the notion of identity.

It should be remarked, however, that, while the Principle of the Identity of Indiscernibles is necessarily applicable to all *substances*, it need not, and should not, be taken as necessarily applicable to *phenomena*.[9] That two like objects might be indistinguishable to humans operating with limited means for observational discrimination could be granted by Leibniz as unproblematic for his system. He does not have to hold that all things are distinguished, but only that they are *distinguishable*—discriminable, in the final analysis, by God, who alone knows the complete individual notions of the substances at issue.

Objecting to the Identity of Indiscernibles principle, Bertrand Russell has argued as follows:

> If a substance is *only* defined by its predicates—and this is essential to the Identity of Indiscernibles—then it would seem to be identical with the sum of those predicates. In that case, to say that such and such a substance exists is merely a compendious ways of saying that all its predicates exist. ... But this ... is not what Leibniz intends to say. The substance is a single simple indivisible thing ... ; it is not the same as the series of its states [predicates], but is the subject of them. But in this case, a substance is not properly speaking *defined* by its predicates.[10]

This counterargument of Russell's breaks down because he refuses to take proper notice of the distinction between *the characterization of a thing* (i.e., the formula that provides its individual defining concept), and *the (corresponding) thing characterized*. The thing is, of course, different from the individual *concept* that defines it (else how could the question of its *creation* arise?), although it answers to it fully, in every respect, since the defining concept provides a *complete* description of the thing defined.[11] The individual concept of a substance is not like a blueprint or an architect's drawing in specifying only an incomplete set of descriptive details about the thing at issue, so that a plurality of items could be made corresponding to the plan. Russell fails to take seriously Leibniz' insistence that the individual concept of a thing be complete and specify every detail about this thing. This is the reason why two or more distinct substances cannot correspond to one individual concept.

4. *Possible Worlds and Logical Truth*

All of the combinatorially feasible, logically possible descriptive combinations for substances do indeed describe some individual, be it actual or merely possible. Thus every potentially contingent possibility is realized in some possible worlds and fails to be realized in some others. Accordingly the only propositions that hold with respect to *all* possible worlds whatsoever are the truths that obtain on grounds of metaphysical necessity: the truths of logic and the conceptually analytical truths. Indeed, such truths are uniquely characterized by the fact that they obtain "in *every* possible world," in contrast with the specifically contingent ones that hold only in *this* possible world, viz., the actual one. In Leibniz' thought, the fact that logical truths obtain in all possible worlds establishes an important linkage between logic and metaphysics.

5. *The Evaluation of Possible Worlds: The Choice of the Best*

Which of the alternative possible worlds he contemplates *sub ratione possibilitatis* is God to select for actualization? This question clearly poses one of the central issues of Leibniz' philosophy. His answer is straightforward: God is to choose *the best* of possible worlds. One difficulty arises at the outset here: Leibniz envisages that an objection can be made to the idea of a "best possible universe" on grounds that it is impossible to conceive of a *best* creature of any kind; it will always be possible to imagine a more perfect one, and so on *ad indefinitum*. This objection, he maintains, is not correct, since it does not apply to the type of "creature" that is an entire universe, and what may hold for an individual substance will not hold for a universe:

> Someone will say that it is impossible to produce the best [possible world] because there is no perfect creature, and that it is always possible to produce one still more perfect. I reply that what can be said of a creature or of a particular substance, which can always be surpassed by another, is not to be applied to the universe, which, since it must extend through all future eternity, is an infinity.[12]

NOTES

1. See *Phil.*, VII, p. 303 (Loemker, p. 487).
2. "God, comparing two simple substances [of the same world] finds present in each grounds which oblige him to accommodate the other to it." (*Monadology*, §52.)
3. *Phil.*, VI, p. 107.
4. *Phil.*, IV, p. 433 (Loemker, p. 308).
5. *Phil.*, VII, p. 393 (Loemker, p. 699).
6. *Ibid.*, p. 219. The principle so formulated might be construed either as the thesis $x = y \equiv (\phi)\phi x \equiv \phi y$ or as the rule: If $x = y$ then from ϕx we may infer ϕy, for any ϕ; and conversely.
7. *Phil.*, VII, p. 372 (4th letter to Clarke, §6).
8. Leibniz' 5th letter to Clarke, §26 cf. §§1–6 of the 4th letter.
9. See Chap. 8.
10. Bertrand Russell, *Critical Exposition*, p. 59.
11. This anticipates a line of argument later espoused by Kant in his *Versuch einiger Betrachtungen über den Optimismus* (1759).
12. *Phil.*, VI, p. 232; *Théodicée*, §195.

Chapter VI

Relations and Incompossibility

1. *The Crucial Role of Incompossibility*

Since the "program" (complete individual notion) of a substance involves the specification of literally every facet of its career, it involves all details of the relation of this substance to others. But now suppose that:

> 1. Possible substance #1 has the property P and also has the property that there is no substance having property Q to which it (#1) stands in the relationship R.
> 2. Possible substance #2 has the property Q and also has the property that every substance having the property P stands in the relationship R to it (#2).

These two substances are patently incompatible (on logical grounds). God might realize #1 or He might realize #2, but He cannot possibly realize both of them. (It is a fundamental tenet of Leibniz' philosophy that even omnipotence cannot accomplish the impossible.) Substances which clash in this way are characterized by Leibniz as *incompossible*. All of the substances comprising any possible world must, of course, be mutually *compossible* in the correlative sense.

The purely logic fact that different possibilities can be mutually incompatible—that not all possibilities will be *compossible* in admitting of concurrent realization—plays a crucial role in Leibniz' metaphysics. It yields the reason why God must unavoidably choose between *alternative* schemes of things, between different possible worlds. The need for such a choice is crucial to God's status as a moral agent. As Leibniz wrote the day after his meeting with Spinoza in 1676:

> If all possibles existed, no reason for existence would be needed and possibility alone would suffice. Therefore there would be no God save insofar as he is possible. But such a God as the pious hold to would not be possible if the opinion of those is true who hold that all possibles exist.[1]

The prospect of incompossible worlds is a logical circumstance that has profound theological implications.

2. *Relational Properties Are Needed for Incompossibility*

If substances were not mutually interrelated there would be no prospect of their incompossibility.

Consider two possible substances defined via their complete individual notions:

a: A_1, A_2, A_3, ...
b: B_1, B_2, B_3, ...

How can an incompatibility arise? Clearly only if we can extract from the conjunction $A_1(a)$ & $A_2(a)$ & $A_3(a)$ & ... the fact that "There is no substance x such that $B_1(x)$ & $B_3(x)$ &. ..." But this conclusion can follow from the $A_1(a)$ conjunction only if this conjunction gives information about a substance distinct from a. information of a kind that involves an essential reference to substances distinct from a.

Leibniz' clear insistence that substances have relational properties—as with "Adam is the father of Cain" or "Caesar married Calpurnia"—is motivated by the consideration that in this way alone can substances be incompossible, as the actual Adam is incompossible with a Noah characterized as (*inter alia*) "the father of Cain."

3. *The Reducibility of Relations*

Leibniz espoused a metaphysical theory of "(real) existence" according to which only substances and their properties are real.[2] Other things—preeminently including *relations* between substances—are merely "things of the mind" (*entia rationis*), mental products belonging to the realm of phenomenal *appearance* rather than that of existential *reality*:

> Therefore we must say that this relation, in this third way of considering it [as something beyond the modifications of the two relata], is indeed *outside* the subjects; but being neither a substance, nor an accident, it must be a merely ideal thing, the consideration of which is nevertheless useful.[3]

How can this insistence on the *ideality* of relations be reconciled with their indispensable role in underwriting incompossibility?

The answer is that relations—while from a certain point of view "ideal" —nevertheless have a solid foothold in undoubted reality, in the properties of substances. Indeed a relation only "exists" insofar as it roots in the properties of its relata. Relations do not have reality in their own right, but a dependent reality correlative with their reducibility to substantial properties. Let us consider how this Leibnizian doctrine is to be understood.

Consider, to begin with, the relational thesis

Titius is wiser than Caius.

It substance-descriptive foundation lies in the two predicative facts:

Caius is somewhat wise.
Titius is very wise.

To these we must conjoin certain "universal truths," namely the general (definitionally guaranteed) facts:

1. wiser = superior in point of wisdom
2. "very" represents a degree superior to "somewhat."

The predicative facts clearly suffice for extracting the substantival relation at issue (given universal truths).[4]

Unfortunately, matters are not always so simple. Relation need not always boil down to *conjunctions* of predicative facts. Sometimes more complex modes of compounding are necessary.

Take the relational fact "Adam is the father of Cain." Leibniz maintains that this reduces to the fact that (1) Adam has two properties

1. Being a father
2. Being a father in virtue of (*propter*)
   Cain's being a son

and (2) the fact that Cain has the two properties:

1. Being a son
2. Being a son in virtue of Adam's being a father.[5]

The relation (relational fact) in question, namely "Adam is the father of Cain," thus issues from a series of predicational facts about the relata, predictational facts in which, to be sure, a compounding operator—the reason-adducing "in virtue of" (*eo ipso* or *propter*) connective—plays a role.[6]

And Leibniz holds that this circumstance is perfectly general. Whenever a relation obtains between two substances, i.e., aRb, there will have to be purely descriptive (i.e., *nonrelational*) properties P and Q such that aRb is logically equivalent with the conjunction $[Pa \ \& \ (Pa \ @ \ Qb)] \ \& \ [Qb \ \& \ (Qb \ @ \ Pa)]$, where @ stands for "is attributable to" (i.e., represents the *eo ipso* or *propter* connective). In this way *relations will always inhere in the nonrelational properties of the relata at issue* through the linking mediation of a syncategorematic connective. And this indicates another basis for construing relations as things of the mind—the fundamental *propter* reason-why grounding which serves as a rationale-presenting device is fundamentally mind-oriented.

Accordingly, a relation has no existence of its own, over and above that of the related substances and their (nonrelational) properties. The complete descriptions afford (predicational) information about the substances of a possible world sufficient always to make it possible to obtain by derivation all the facts about relationships as well. A relation has no standing apart from the existence of the relata and their properties. It is nowise a *tertium quid* existing on its own, independently of the relata. A relationship is a compound of predicative facts, but not anything further with an independent factual status of its own. Construed in terms of a connecting linkage that is distinct from the items it links, it lies wholly in the mind of the beholder.

The correlativity of relational and predicational facts, and the pervasiveness of the connection of rationale-provision inherent in the Principle of Sufficient Reason, means that *every* predication ultimately has relational involvements:

> [T]here is no term so absolute or so loose as not to include relations and the perfect analysis of which does not lead to other things and even to all others; so you can say that relative terms indicate *expressly* the relations they contain [while nonrelative terms merely do so *implicitly*].[7]

All predicative truths have relational ramifications. The pervasiveness of relations is inherent in the fundamental Leibnizian principle *tout est lié* ("Everything is interconnected") with which we dealt in the preceding chapter.

Leibniz accordingly does not teach that relational statements are meaningless, or that intersubstantial relations do not exist, but that all relations that can obtain between substances must inhere in their predicates. Relations are "the work of the mind" (in Russell's phrase) because, when substances are under discussion, relational statements are never "ultimate facts," they are always derivative consequences—"confused" consequences, as Leibniz has it—of conjunctions of predications. For Leibniz, relational statements about substances can never afford information about them that is not given more fully and adequately by a suitable complex of predications.

Accordingly, relational statements are true precisely when they are "well founded" in the properties of the substances at issue.[8] Thus Leibniz writes:

> You will not, I believe, admit an accident which is in two subjects at once. Thus I hold, as regards relations, that paternity in David is one thing, and filiation in Solomon another, but the relation common to both is a merely mental thing, of which the modifications of singulars are the foundation.[9]

Different substances do not share the same modification: paternity in David is *fatherhood of Solomon*, paternity in Adam is *fatherhood of Cain and Abel*, and these are quite different. Relations are founded on the "modifications of singulars" and incompossibility results when these go awry: when the Solomon of a world has paternity-of-David whereas its David lacks fatherhood-by-Solomon, for example.

4. *Incompossible Substances*

It is clear now how one must proceed in endeavoring to answer, on Leibniz' behalf, the question: How can the complete individual notions of two individually possible substances *a* and *b* be so constituted as to render them mutually incompossible? One begins with two crucial observations:

> (1) "being related by R to b [i.e., to any substance answering to b's description]" is one of the relational properties of *a*. i.e., *a* has $(\lambda x)xRb$.

and further

> (2) "not standing in the relation R to *a* [i.e., to any substance answering to *a*'s description] is one of the relational properties of *b*, i.e., *b* has $(\lambda x) \sim aRx$.

These two are clearly incompossible, seeing that (1) entails aRb whereas (2) entails $\sim aRb$. Two individuals x and y can only be pairwise compossible if their complete individual notions are such that in each case where one of them has the relational properties of R-ing the other, this other has the relational property of being-R'd by the former.

It is important to recognize, however, that even if such (partially described) substances are *pairwise* compossible, they might still prove to be incompossible *in toto*. For suppose that *a*, *b*, and *c* are such that

> 1. *a* has (*inter alia*) the factor of "being unique in lacking P"[10]
> 2. *b* has (*inter alia*) the factor of "being unique in lacking Q"
> 3. *c* has (*inter alia*) the factor of "being unique in point of

having a lack/possession status for *P* different from that it has for *Q*."

Here any two of these individuals will be mutually compossible. But when all three are put together, their conjoint realization in a single world will clearly be infeasible. However, when we shift from *partially* described substances to complete individual notions this sort of situation does not arise. Substantival compossibility now becomes transitive. For here we have a "block universe" where everything is inseparably connected with everything else. When Adam sins, all mankind comes to reflect his sinfulness.

Their ability to constitute a possible world—their *synoptic* compossibility—is a global and comprehensively systematic feature of a group of possible individuals. Each substance within a possible world carries within itself an ineradicable imprint of all the rest:

[E]very individual substance expresses its whole universe in its own manner, and in its [complete individual] notion is included all of its doings together with all their attendant circumstances and the entire course of exterior occurrences.[11]

None of its substances can be abstracted from that world and none adjoined to it without undoing the intricately woven fabric of compossibility relationships.

5. *Russell's Criticisms of Leibniz on Relations*

In his important study of Leibniz' philosophy Bertrand Russell imputes to Leibniz the thesis that, as he puts it, relations are "*merely* ideal," and then goes on to argue that Leibniz cannot consistently adopt this view:

But as applied to relations, [there is] in Leibniz' case, a special absurdity, namely, that the relational propositions, which God is supposed to know, must be strictly meaningless. The only ground for denying the independent reality of relations is, that propositions must have a subject and a predicate. If this· be so, a proposition without a subject and a predicate must be no proposition, and must be destitute of meaning. But it is just such a proposition which, in the case of ... relations between monads, God is supposed to see and believe. God, therefore, [for Leibniz] believes in the truth of what is meaningless.[12]

Let us evaluate these criticisms. Consider first Russell's objections about God's knowledge of relational statements: "Does God know about the intersubstantial relations?" *Yes and no! Yes:* He knows the predicational facts on which such relations must rest because He knows all genuine facts. *Yes:* He knows that some substances are related to others in their perceptions because this is represented in their own predicates. *No:* He does not know relational facts "from within," i.e., confusedly without explicit awareness of their predicational basis.

Think of recent discussions of the question, "Can God know what is happening now?" He can know what is happening at 3:30 p.m. on Friday, May 3, 1965, or what is happening contemporaneously with my making of this gesture, but He cannot differentiate one "now" from another—to know what occurs in time from the relational perspective of one positioned within the framework. God cannot know temporal facts from the dis-vantage point of one located *within* the framework. He could never entertain the statement, "It is *now* 3:30 p.m. Friday, May 3, 1965"; but that does not mean that there are any temporal facts, relating to the events or occurrences that go on in time, that God does not know.

Russell is thus wrong in saying that, in Leibniz' view, God cannot possibly know relational propositions. He does know them, because he knows the system of predicational facts upon which, in Leibniz' view, all true relational propositions must rest. Precisely because all relational facts about substances are inherent in predications, God lacks no information that true relational statements could conceivably convey. He does not, to be sure, think relationally; He simply connects predictions. But He loses nothing by this since there are, in Leibniz' view, no irreducible relational facts about substances for Him to miss. To say that He misses the confused informational perspective of the limited substances is like saying that He lacks information about intoxication because He does not drink.

In fact, there is a most serious confusion present in Russell's criticism of Leibniz: his charge that for Leibniz, as an adherent to subject-predicate logic, every proposition without a subject and a predicate "must be no proposition, and must be desitute of meaning." This is clearly a gross blunder. Even the most rigid subject-predicate logician is willing to countenance statements of the type, "The sugar is white *and* the salt is white," "The terrace is wet *because* the water-jug is broken"—complex statements in which predicational statements are conjoined, disjoined, or otherwise linked by syncategorematic terms. The subject-predicate logician need not (and Leibniz does not) claim a relational statement as meaningless because there is no way of reformulating it as a solitary subject-predicate statement. He can, exactly as

Leibniz, regard such statements as combinations of predication-statements. Leibniz will, of course, grant Russell that "there are (meaningful) propositions which do not have a subject and a predicate," but will do so without abandoning his commitment to the subject-predicate prototype. He takes the position that, in the particular case of propositions about the things of this world, such complex propositions must be capable of being extracted from subject-predicate statements duly *combined* by means of syncategorematic terms (such as the *ep ipso* relationship of reason-why grounding).

NOTES

1. Couturat, *Opuscules*, p. 530; Loemker, p. 169; compare Loemker, p. 263.
2. This is essentially the doctine of Avicenna (and the Arabic Aristotelians in general) who held that everything real is either substance or attribute. (See Julius Weinberg, *Abstraction, Relation, and Induction* [Madison: University of Wisconsin Press, 1965].) To be sure, these ideas undoubtedly reached Leibniz via the schoolmen (especially Aquinas and Scotus).
3. Fifth letter to Clarke, §47.
4. For more on Leibniz' theory of relations see Benson Mates, "Leibniz on Possible Worlds" in H .G. Frankfurt (ed.), *Leibniz: A Collection of Critical Essays* (New York, 1972), pp. 335–64. (Some of the other essays in this volume are also relevant.)
5. However, we must here construe such generic "relations" as *being a father* or *being a son*, where no specific relatum is at issue, as predicative in nature.
6. Sometimes Leibniz assigns this task to a "since" or "seeing that" connective, specifically *quantenus*. Or again sometimes to a "thereby" (*ep ipso*) construed as "Adam is a father and thereby (*ep ipso*) Cain is a son." All these are variations on the same reason-giving theme of a fundamentally syncategorematic *ratio-essendi* specifying connective conjoining strictly predicational facts. What is at issue is not a *relation between things* but a *relationship between facts*. For further details regarding Leibniz' approach see G.H.R. Parkinson, *Logic and Reality in Leibniz' Metaphysics* (Oxford, 1965), pp. 39–52.
7. *Nouv. Ess.*, Bk. II, chap. 25, §10 (bracketed internal added).
8. We have been dealing throughout this chapter with relations between *substances* (monadic relations). Relations among (well founded) phenomena are, of course, also held to be reducible by Leibniz, doubly so because they reduce to inter-monadic relations which then, in turn, come to be grounded in the properties of the several substances involved. Some interesting observations on phenomenal relations occur in *Nouv. Ess.*, Bk. II, chap. 11, §§4ff.
9. *Phil.*, II, p. 486; Loemker, p. 992.
10. That is, *a* has the relational property that "apart from myself, no individual in my world environment has *P*."
11. *Discourse on Metaphysics*, §9.
12. Russell, *Critical Exposition*, pp. 14–15.

Chapter VII

Some Key Principles of the Contingent Sphere

1. *Preliminaries*

This chapter will deal with three important principles of contingence—subsidiaries of the Principle of Perfection—which play a prominent part in Leibniz' philosophy. Since they hinge upon the Principle of Perfection, these principles hold only in the *actual* world, that is, the best possible one. They serve to characterize this world and distinguish it from other, inherently inferior possible worlds.

2. *The Principle of Plenitude*

The Principle of Perfection has it that the world as a whole is as perfect as possible, that God actualized that possible world in which perfection is at a maximum. God is perfect, consequently the only outlet for that perfection—the world—is as perfect as it is possible for a world to be. There are not, as with Descartes, partial imperfections compensated for by the perfection of the whole. Each part of the world aids in the maximization of perfection by contributing the maximum of perfection possible for it. Within the limits of possibility, the actual world accordingly contains the most perfection. It suffices only to add the premise that existence is a mode of perfection to obtain as consequence of Leibniz' thesis that the actual world is such that the "quantity of existence" is maximized within the "best of possible worlds."

There is thus in Leibniz' metaphysics, a Principle of Plenitude—that is, of "existence-maximization"—that is linked to, and indeed immediately derivative from, the Principle of Perfection.

3. *The Law of Continuity*

The notion of continuity has application wherever a concept of *nearness* is provided, and the question *Do the objects in the neighborhood of a given object possess such and such a property?* can be raised meaningfully.[1] Leibniz formulated this through the idea that, when in the solution of problems the differences in data diminish, so do the differences in the results obtained from these data; when the former go to zero the latter follow suit. This principle, Leibniz maintains, "depends on a yet more general principle, namely: as the data ordered, so the unknowns are ordered also."[2]

In 1687 Leibniz formulated a metaphysical principle based on such mthematical considerations. He characterized the fact that physical nature everywhere exhibits such continuities in its laws of operation as the Law of Continuity (*lex continuitatis*).[3] Throughout its presentations[4], this Law of Continuity was presented by Leibniz as a consequence of the Principle of Perfection. The derivation is based on the line of thought that, by embodiment of continuity among its constituents, a possible world exhibits one of the modes of perfection.

The application for the sake of which the first formulation in the principle took place was the revelation of an error in the laws of motion as given by Descartes.[5] As usual when he is in possession of a useful mathematical or physical principle, Leibniz applies it in philosophy, where it is given the formulation: "Jumps are forbidden not only in motions, but also in every order of things and of truths."[6] Let us consider some instances of continuity and applications of the continuity principle of Leibniz' philosophy.

A. *Continuity in the realm of monads*

1. From the very first the monad is presented as a perduring substance.[7] In mathematical jargon a one-parameter family of states is involved,[8] and this change of state of a substance (appetition) is continuous.

2. At any instant every monad represents the entire universe from its own point of view with varying degrees of clarity. This makes possible a twofold continuous distribution of the monads. (a) In *point of view*—it is always possible to find a monad differing from a given monad in point of view by less than any preassigned difference. This is basic to the Leibnizian theory of space, and to his denial of a vacuum.[9] (b) In *perfection*[10]—determined in terms of clarity of perception, the varying degrees of which thus effect a continuous ordering of the system of monads.[11]

3. The monads are also continuously ordered with regard to *structure*. As Russell puts it, "If two substances differ by a finite difference there must be a continuous series of intermediate substances, each of which differs infinitesimally from the next."[12] In this way Leibniz denies what he terms a "vacuum formarum."[13]

Thus continuity enters in Leibniz' metaphysical world in monadic structure, viewpoint, appetition, and perfection.

B. *Continuity in the physical world*

1. The monadic aggregates of the physical world are of two kinds, those well founded phenomena that are no more than mere phenomena, and "true unities." The aggregates with unity, the living beings,[14] are continuously ordered with respect to the perfection of their dominant monad. All creatures are linked in a "liaison universelle."[15] This leads also to the continuity of the species of living beings.[16]

2. It proceeds from considerations concerning monads that physical space is a plenum.[17] This is mentioned here in passing, for we shall have more to say later about the nature of physical space as conceived by Leibniz.

3. The ancient theory of atoms and the void—as resurrected in modern times by Hobbes, Gassendi, and others—can be ruled out on continuity considerations. The existence of atoms would contradict the continuities of nature.[18]

4. All the processes of the physical world (motion, impact, and so on) take place continuously, according to Leibniz.[19] To put the matter as briefly as possible, the principle of continuity as applied to the physical world underwrites the classical principle *natura non facit saltus.*

C. *Other occurrences of continuity in the philosophy of Leibniz*

The famous doctrine of the "little perceptions" plays a key role in Leibniz' theory of knowledge and in his psychology. As a corollary to this doctrine the continuity of life in sleep, unconsciousness, and even in death is obtained. The little perceptions are also invoked to explain the continuity of change in conscious thought. Using them as a starting point, Leibniz establishes an elaborate psychology involving "petites dégagements," and an "inquiétude" composed of "petites solicitations."[20] By means of these the continuity of the passions is demonstrated; for example, just as rest is an infinitesimal motion so joy is an infinitesimal sorrow.[21] The principle of continuity is thoroughly diffused throughout the philosophy of Leibniz.[22]

Regarding the Law of Continuity, Russell writes: "This law usually holds a prominent place in expositions of Leibniz, but I cannot discover that, except as applied to Mathematics, it has any great importance."[23] Such slight valuation of the principle of continuity is misguided, for the principle not only holds a prominent place in expositions of Leibniz, it holds one in the metaphysical system of Leibniz as well. Indeed, it provides, as we shall see, one of the fundamental bases for Leibniz' entire theory of space and time, and moreover is, as we have seen, central to his psychological theory.

4. *The Pre-Established Harmony* (Harmonia Rerum)

Leibniz splits the realm of the actual into two domains: the realm of monads, the real world, which forms the object of study of metaphysics; and the realm of the things of our everyday experience, the phenomenal world, which forms the object of study of the sciences in general, but pre-eminently of physics. These two realms, physical and metaphysical, are not disparate or disjoint, but are different aspects of the same world. The system of phenomena results from the system of monads, and is well founded in it.

The notion of well founding, and the several theories by which it is implemented, occupies a central position in Leibniz' thought. Here, at the joining of physics and metaphysics, we shall have occasion later for detailed investigations. At the moment let it suffice to remark that the main instrument for well founding, providing the means for explaining phenomena in terms of monads, is the pre-established harmony. It explains how similarities and uniformities arise among monads, and thus accounts for the behaviour of monadic aggregates, and for their relation to individual monads.

A word must be said concerning the pre-established harmony in its own right. It is a *harmony* that obtains among the monads, not a mutual causal influence, because every individual substance is self-complete, and its development in time is fixed. Monads are *windowless*; they neither admit nor emit any causal impetus. No causal relations can arise among monads; at best they can *accord* with one another in their states. This protocausal reciprocal accord extends throughout the universe and links all of its monads in one vast framework of mutual interrelation. We humans lose sight of this

because our senses lead us to judge only superficially, but in reality, because of the interconnection of things, the entire universe, with all of its parts, would be wholly different, and would have been another world altogether from its very commencement, if the least thing in it happened otherwise than it has.[24]

This accord is *pre*-established in a dual sense: first because it is determined upon anterior to the creation of the world, second because the accord at any instant of time is but the consequence of the accord at any previous instant. These interconnections are of an intimate linkage that continues operative in infinite detail throughout the course of historical development of the universe:

> All singular things [i.e., substances] are successive ... nor is there anything permanent in them, on my view, except that law itself which involves this continued succession, agreeing in singulars with [all] that which is in the whole universe.[25]

The fact that the actual world is such that a thoroughgoing network of agreement and accord obtains among its constituents is not a necessary result. It represents a mode of perfection of this world, not an inevitable feature of every possible world. It is a contingent truth—one that obtains by virtue of the Principle of Perfection—that a Pre-Established Harmony reigns among the constituent substances of the actual world.

It is important for an understanding of Leibniz to distinguish between *compossibility*—mutual linkage and accommodation of the purely logical sort at issue with conceptual consonance—and *harmony* proper, mutual attunement within an orderly system. The mutual compossibility of the substances within this actual world, and/or of those within any other possible one, is a metaphysically necessary feature. This purely logical mutual accord of world-coordinate substances in the minimal sense of mutual comptibility is logically inevitable. But the fact that is substances harmonize with one another in a manner far beyond mere logical compatibility to make for an intricately articulated system, a genuine *cosmos* (a world governed by simple, general, and universal laws of physical and psychological order) is something quite different. And it is this feature which serves to mark this as "the best possible world." Logical compossibility and nomic harmony are very different matters, the former a necessary feature of every world, the latter a contingent feature of the real one.

*   *   *

It deserves stress that the constellation of principles considered here indicates that Leibniz can claim for his own metaphysical system the sort of perfection at issue in his ontology itself: richness of detail articulated within a unifying framework of principles of order.

NOTES

1. The continuity properties of functions play an important role in mathematical analysis, and there is little doubt that it was his mathematical studies which suggested to Leibniz the philosophic potentialities of the continuity concept.

2. *Phil.*, III, p. 52 (Loemker, p. 351). Cf. also the opuscule tr. in P.P. Wiener, *Leibniz: Selections* (New York: Charles Scribner's Sons, 1951), pp. 65–70.

3. "Lex continuitatis" or "principle de continuite." See *Phil.*, III, pp. 51–5 (Loemker, pp. 351–3 [1687]); *Math.*, VII, pp. 260 ff., esp. 266–71 (probably 1687); and also Couturat, *Logique*, p. 398, n. It is conceivable that Leibniz had continuity considerations in mind when he rejected the perfectly elastic impact of *particles*, and hence atomism, since a discontinuity is involved here. The time of this rejection, the stay in Paris, adds plausibility to this.

4. Its invocations as an explicit philosophical principle commenced ca. 1687.

5. Leibniz described continuity as a useful principle of invention in physics, and also as a very convenient test to see if certain given rules actually work. Phil., III, p. 52 (Loemker, p. 351 ff.).

6. *Ibid.*, p. 635 (Loemker, p. 658).

7. See DM and the correspondence with Arnauld.

8. "The complete or perfect notion (concept) of a singular (individual) substance involves all its predicates, past, present, and future." (Couturat, *Opuscules*, p. 520.).

9. Consequently we find Leibniz saying that the monads are ordered "comme autant d'Ordonnées d'une même Courbe, dont l'union ne souffre pas, qu'on place d'autres entre deux, à cause que cela marqueroit du désordre et de l'imperfection" [Guhrauer, *Leibniz*, Vol. I (Breslau: F. Hirt, 1846), Anmerkungen, p. 32].

10. I.e., in clarity of perception or adequacy of representation. See *Phil.*, VII, p. 535.

11. "All singular [L has *individual*] created substances are diverse expressions of the same universe, but the expressions vary in perfection." Cp. *Phil.* II, p. 136.

12. Russell, *Critical Exposition*, p. 64–5.

13. *Phil.*, VI, p. 548; *Phil.*, II, p. 168; *Nouv Ess.*, II, Chap 4, §13.

14. For present purposes we can adopt the view held by Leibniz in some passages that all animals, even the lowest, may be regarded as true unities.

15. *Phil.*, IV, p. 546; *Nouv. Ess.*, IV, Chap. 21, §12.

16. Guhrauer, *op. cit.*, p. 32–3.

17. Cf. *Monadology*, §§66–9.

18. *Math.*, II, p. 156.

19. See, for example, the discussion of motion in Leibniz' *Dynamica* (*Math.*, VI, pp. 320–6).

20. *Nouv. Ess.*, II, Chap. 20, §6.

21. See G. Wanke, *Das Stetigkeitsgesetz bei Leibniz* (Kiel: Universitäts-druckerei, 1892), especially p. 30.

22. "Francis of Borgia, General of the Jesuits, who has at last been canonized, being wont to drank largely when he was a man in high life, reduced himself little by little upon a small scale, when he thought of retiring (from the world) by causing a drop of wax to fall daily into the bottle which he was wont to empty" (*Nouv. Ess.*, II, Chap. 21, §31; tr. Langley, p. 193).

23. Russell, *Critical Exposition*, p. 63.

24. *Phil.*, II, p. 52 (Loemker, p. 334).

25. *Phil.*, II, p. 263 (Loemker, p. 534).

Chapter VIII

The Realm of Monads and its Creation

1. *How the Realm of Monads Differ from Other Possible Worlds*

Leibniz held that the actual world, the realm of created monads, is but one of infinitely many possible worlds. It is, however, a very special one, the alternative uniquely qualified for realization or actualization (actual creation) on the basis of its possession of a certain special feature—its maximal perfection as determined by two factors: its *variety*, manifested in the richness of its phenomena, and its *orderliness*, manifested in the simplicity of its laws. In view of its perfection the actual world exhibits in great measure three features which Leibniz—as we have just seen—regards as having central importance: *plenitude, continuity,* and *harmony.* Its possession of such modes of order in a relatively greater degree than all other possible worlds that are even close to ours in contentual richness serves to set the actual world apart from its possible competitors.

The continuity and harmony inherent in the design of the actual world assure that it exhibits orderliness at both a private and a public level of consideration. At the *individual* level, each single monad, considered individually, exhibits continuity and harmony entering into the assemblage of mutually contemporaneous factors which constitute one specific state of a monad, and into the state-to-state transition (appetition) characteristic of monadic change; there is no passage from state to state without intervening passage through the intermediate states. At the *general* level, continuity and harmony again enter into the entire system of monads in the constitution of mutually contemporaneous states which constitute an intermonadic "time-slice" running across the system of monads, and in the macro-changes in monadic complexes. This summary characterization is but a rough sketch that needs development and refinement.

2. *Monadic Perceptions and Their Transition (i.e., Appetition)*

Leibniz' conceives an individual substance as a spatiotemporal continuant, an existent without spatial parts, but not without attributes, and with a perduring individuality and an inner dynamic of change. The state of affairs corresponding to a *consistent* total description of the attributes of a substance may be designated as the *state* of the substance at a given moment. One can be certain that this description characterizes an instaneous (contemporaneous) state of the substance for, as we shall see, the family of attributes of a substance is in constant flux, and its attribute-family over a noninstantaneous period in the history of a substance would be logically inconsistent. That a monad, a substance within the actual world, has innumerably many different states is an aspect of variety; that these states form a continuous and smooth transitional sequence is an aspect of orderliness.

The internal programming of the monads built into their complete individual notion (as into that of every other possible substance) is the basis for the state-to-state transition that makes them unstable and ever-changing. This feature of monads—of so changing that each of its new states is but a prelude to others—leads Leibniz to the metaphor that "the present is pregnant with the future." Each individual substance is subject to a perpetual change of state; such changes are without jumps, the transition of the substance from one state to another being always continuous.

It should be remarked that having many states, and distinct states at distinct "times," is a logically necessary feature of every possible substance (derived partly from the very concept of a possible substance itself, and partly from the Principle of the Identity of Indiscernibles). However, the contingent fact that monadic change is smooth and orderly—i.e., continuous—and, more generally, that the world is a harmonious *cosmos*, not a *chaos*, is inherent in the Principle of Perfection. It is a matter not just of *correlation* but of *coordination* and mutual accommodation. (If the instruments of an orchestra were to play different pieces, correlation is still possible, but the result is not music but cacophony.) The states of a monad, seeing that they reflect its accomodation to those of the others, may be characterized as its *perceptions*.

Continuous change from one system of perceptions to another is the only "activity" of which an individual substance is capable.[1] Leibniz chooses to call it *appetition*, defining it as "the tendency from one perception to another,"[2] but the dangerous connotations of this term in the direction of active, and above all *conscious*, seeking or striving must be avoided. The duality, reminiscent of the curve-equations in Cartesian coordinates, of the "law of development," and the development itself, are deeply ingrained into

Leibniz' concept of appetition. His retention of both intensional and extensional interpretations of logic is significant for his theory of individual substance as involving both a *determinative conception* or *law* (the complete individual notion) and the *continuing series* of concrete particular events or perceptions which are the instantiations of this concept.

3. *Perception and Representation*

One of the consequences of the pre-established harmony is that to any instantaneous state of a given individual substance there corresponds exactly one smoothly accordant state of every other individual substance. Such an instantaneous "contemporaneity-slice" cutting through the history of all substances defines a moment of *time*. (The time-order of the universe is a feature of this best possible world, not a logically necessary feature of any possible world as such.) Thus at any moment of time each substance "perceives" or "represents" or "expresses" all the others, in the sense that a certain similarity relationship obtains between their states. Thus clarity of perception represents harmonization as well.

"Representation" is, for Leibniz, the inverse of *perception*: *A* is represented in *B* insofar as *B* perceives *A*. Substantial light can thus be shed upon monadic preception from the angle of Leibniz' representation in the following terms:

> One thing *expresses* another, in my use of the term, when there is a constant and regulated relation between what can be said [i.e., *predicated*] of the one and of the other. It is thus that a projection in perspective expresses a geometric figure.[3]

Things thus represent one another, to the extent that a structural agreement obtains between them. This is not a strictly reciprocal matter, like ordinary similarity, because one represents the other more fully than the reverse when the structure they commonly exhibit is more clearly and distinctly defined in one than in the other.

The universal correspondence established by the mutual perceptions of substances is not the result of causal interaction, but of a divinely ordained accord, the pre-established harmony.[4] Each substance is not "represented" or "perceived" or "expressed" by every other substance in an equally sharp and detailed way. There are varying degrees of clarity, and inversely of confusion, in "perception," and so, as Leibniz graphically put it, "every mind is omniscent but confused."[5] Every monad perceives all others, but each perceives more clearly those substances closer to, or more important for, it.[6] Thus each substance perceives the whole universe from its own special point of view, and this is the basis for the spatial relationships among substances. (Note that in this way both spatiality and temporality are a facet of every possible universe which involves a plurality of mutually according substances with changing states, and are not confined to this existing universe.)

Since all monads are fundamentally alike, in that every monad perceives everything else in the universe, a question can be raised as to how they can possibly differ from one another. Leibniz seems to think in terms of the analogy of painting, of two different depictions of exactly the same scene. Monads, he says, differ from one another not in what they perceive, but (1) in *point of view*, i.e., with differing features of the things they perceive; and (2) in *clearness of perception*, i.e., with differing faithfulness of representation of the various aspects of things. Leibniz thus replies to the question of the present paragraph as follows:

> It is not in the objects represented that the monads are limited, but in the modification of their knowledge of the object. In a confused way they all reach out to infinity or to the whole, but are limited and differentiated in the degrees of their distinct perceptions.[7]

Although monadic perception is basically determined in terms of similarity, the relationship at issue is not actually a symmetric one, for certainly monad *A* can perceive monad *B* more clearly than *B* perceives *A*. The best way to think of the matter is in pictographic terms: *A* and *B* perceive the same thing, but *A* perceives it more sharply than *B* does.

Leibniz flatly states that there is nothing whatever to substances over and above concurrent perceptions and their chronological appetitions from one perception to another.[8] Does this mean that a monad has no autonomous properties characteristic of it as such, without being reflective of another? Is the realm of monads a shadow world of perceptions of perceptions of perceptions, *ad indefinitum*, a perpetual being-for-others without any being-of-itself? Of course not! A Leibnizian "perception" is not *merely* other-reflective; it has a strictly internal basis as a matter of *accord* between orthodoxly qualitative properties. The fact that all of a monad's properties agree with those of others does not make all of them into perceptions, but does not prevent them from being—nay, in Leibniz' view *requires* them to be—genuinely internal properties, not simply shadowy reflections of the (equally shadowy) properties of others. The objection at issue *inverts* the true perspective. There is nothing to monads except their *states* (and the succession thereof), and these states are the basis of their mutual perceptions of one another and of a common world.

4. The Creation

Each possible substance possesses a greater or lesser degree of perfection proportionally with its being capable of greater or lesser clarity in perceiving its fellows in the possible world of which it is a member. The merit that qualifies the substance for actualization, its quantity of essence or potentiality for existence, is directly proportional to its perfection. God, desirous to act in the most perfect possible way, actualizes the possible world constituted by that system of possible substances for which the sum total of perfection is at a maximum.

It thus becomes possible to appreciate the general direction of Leibniz' exculpation of God from blame for evil and imperfection as they seem to exist in the world. Each substance has "always" subsisted, or, strictly speaking, has had a conceptual mode of being that lies outside of time altogether—*sub ratione possibilitalis*. Its total nature was determined, for its adequate and complete notion (including all its predicates save *existence*) was fixed.[9] For this nature God is in no way responsible; it is an object of his understanding, and no creature of his will. The limits of possibility are an inescapable limitation upon all power—even divine omnipotence. God cannot do the impossible. As John Stuart Mill rightly observed with respect to the *Theodicée*:

> In every page of the work [Leibniz] tacitly assumes an abstract possibility and impossibility, independent of the divine power: and though his pious feelings make him continue to designate that power by the word Omnipotence, he so explains that term as to make it mean, power extending to all that is within the limits of that abstract possibility.[10]

God chose the best (i.e., most perfect) system of compossible substances for actualization, thus he is the reason for all existence, hence for all existent perfection and imperfection. Yet this leaves no room for reproach and represents no derogation of perfection. For imperfection is not avoidable since, by the identity of indiscernibles, no substance different from God can be wholly perfect. God, however, chose to minimize imperfection, or rather, positively, to maximize perfection. He is positively the cause of existent perfection, but only negatively of imperfection, since he retained only what could not but remain. This is how Leibniz accounts for imperfection in the best of all possible worlds.

On the basis of God's own perfection, each possible substance has a "claim" to existence in accordance with its own perfection and that of its possible world, a claim which correspondingly endows it with a "drive towards existence."

Commenting on Leibniz' statement that "One can define an existent as that which is compatible more than anything else which is incompatible with it,"[11] Russell holds that:

> Strange consequences follow if Leibniz intended this to be, in a strict sense, a definition of "existence." For, if it was so intended there was no act of Creation. ... This world, it would follow, exists by definition without the need of any Divine Decree.[12]

Since Leibniz held that existence cannot be accounted for without a reliance upon divine decrees, the above is not, strictly speaking. to be taken as a definition at all. Its status in the logical development of Leibniz' system is that of a *theorem*, i.e., a derivative principle. It is, in fact, an immediate corollary of the Principle of Perfection—a principle obtaining in virtue of a divine decree. Thus Russell is right that, strictly speaking, there is no *definition* at issue here.

Leibniz sometimes speaks incautiously on this issue. In one passage he writes:

> [T]here is in possible things, or in possibility or essence itself, some exigency of existence, or, so to speak, a reaching out for existence, or, in a word, ... essence itself tends toward existence. Whence it follows that all possibles, i.e., things expressing essence or possible reality, tend by equal rights toward existence, according to the quality of essence in reality, or the degree of perfection which they involve.[13]

It must be stressed that such statements take a drastic shortcut in leaving God out of the picture. For the "exigency of existence" at issue is only operative insofar as *claims on God's consideration* are at issue. (Compare pp. 33–34 above.)

Russell is also right in holding that it is difficult to find a place in Leibniz' cosmology for an historical "act" of creation; Leibniz' *creation* can in no sense be an *historical* event. There was no moment of time when the universe was not, for time itself is logically posterior to the existence of the universe. Further, an act of creation would seem to require a first instant in the history of the thing created, and Leibniz, though he inclines toward the view that there is a first moment of time, is by no means dogmatic on this point.[14] Had Leibniz conceived of the creation in a quasi-historical fashion, he would doubtless have been firmer about this. We thus arrive at the conclusion that Leibniz regarded God as a necessary condition for the existence of a world, but that it would be an error to attribute to him any view of an historical act of creation. To speak of anything as *prior* to the existent universe is to use the term in a purely logical, not temporal sense. Most of the building blocks of Leibniz' metaphysic are timeless. For here one deals with the necessary being, the necessary truths, and the possible worlds, entering the sphere of pure concepts, where it is difficult to find a place for activity of any sort, save through the door provided by the concept of activity itself.

NOTES

1. Compare pp. 79–80 below.
2. *Phil.*, III, p. 575 (Loemker, p. 663).
3. *Phil.*, II, p. 112 (Loemker, p. 339).
4. Given the omnidetermination of its complete individual notion, a substance cannot be acted upon by another in the usual phase of the bringing about of something that would not otherwise be.
5. L. Couturat, *Opuscules*, p. 10.
6. For the principles governing the clarity of perception see *Phil.*, II, p. 90, and *Monadology*, §60.
7. *Monadology*, §60.
8. "... nothing but this—namely perceptions and their changes—can be found in a simple substance" (*Monadology*, §17). "... any one Monad in itself and at a particular moment can be distinguished from any other only by internal qualities and activities, which cannot be other than its *perceptions* (that is to say, the representation of the compound, or of that which is outside, in the simple) and its *appetitions* (that is to say, its tendencies to pass from one perception to another), which are the principles of change" (PNG, §2).
9. "The complete or perfect notion of a singular substance involves all its predicates, past, present, and future" (Couturat, *Opuscules*, p. 520; cf. *ibid.*, p. 403). That existence is not among these predicates follows from the fact that the complete notion of possible substances was completely determined and accessible to the mind of God anterior to any decisions of creation (cf. *Phil.*, II, p. 50; Loemker, p. 333). It is, therefore, clear that existence, if a predicate at all for Leibniz, is a very exceptional one, which cannot in the nature of things enter into the complete individual notion (essence) of any substance save God alone. (Compare §5 of Chap. II above, and also fn. 3 of Chap. XIV.)
10. Quoted in John Hick, *Evil and the God of Love* (New York: Harper & Row, 1966), p. 171.

11. Couturat, *Opuscules*, p. 360.

12. Russell, *Critical Exposition*, p. vi.

13. *Phil.*, VII, p. 303.

14. The later chapter on Leibniz' theories of space and time will present evidence for these statements.

Chapter IX

Well Founding and Monadic Aggregation

1. *The Concept of "Well Founding" and its Role in Leibniz' System*

Leibniz holds that only individual substances—monads—can be considered genuinely real. For these alone are authentic units of existence (be it actual or possible), and Leibniz espoused the scholastic maxim *ens et unum convertuntur:* what is not truly *one* being is thereby not truly a *being.*[1] Accordingly, whatever sorts of *composites* may be formed by monads will not themselves be authentic individuals in their own right. But this is not the end of the matter. For composites may, under certain circumstances, be in a position to make good partially—in some degree at least—their claims to be genuine things, possessing features on their own account, rather than merely phenomenal aspects. Leibniz' conception of *well founding* plays a critical role here.

For Leibniz, a *phenomenon* arises whenever something *appears to* a monad so that it is "represented" in its perceptions. If the condition of things thus to be found in the monad's state corresponds to the conditions actually obtaining in "the external world," i.e., the remaining system of monads, the phenomenon is said to be well founded; when not, the phenomenon is a "mere phenomenon" without an adequate basis in the monadic realm, and therefore of the status of idiosyncratic illusion or delusion. The class of phenomena is much-inclusive, but Leibniz is perfectly prepared to draw, wholly *within* the "phenomenal" sphere, the familiar, common-sense distinction between the real and the imaginary (much as we might distinguish within the perceptual sphere between genuine oasis-sightings and mere mirages).[2] He draws this distinction in terms of a distinction between *mere* phenomenon on the one hand and *real* or *well-founded* on the other.

With a metaphysical system such as Leibniz', as with any scientific account of the world by a process of explanatory "reduction" to some ultimate type of thing that is not encountered in common experience, e.g., atoms, force, or energy, the question of explanatory adequacy arises. The factor (or factors) held by the theory to be "ultimately real" must, somehow, give rise to all there is. The instrumentality through which Leibniz achieves this objective is his concept of *well founding*. It is his rule (which he seemingly never formulated in the abstract, but constantly applied) that the objects with which one deals in the sciences and the phenomena which confront one in everyday life result from properties of the monads that constitute larger-scale aggregates. This principle of well founding can be said to assert that all characteristics of the phenomena are well founded in the monadic realm in the sense of being strictly *derivative* from monadic characteristics.

The philosophical importance of this principle lies on the surface—it represents the effort of a philosophy which separates the world into appearance and reality to achieve genuine unity between these disparate elements. Any such philosophy must face the question: How does reality give rise to the appearances? Leibniz' concept of well founding accordingly embodies the claim that the theory of monads can resolve this question.

2. *Monadic Aggregates: The Basis of Real Phenomena*

In the system of Leibniz, the monad is the building-block of the universe. Exactly as in the classical atomic theory that all things of the world about us result from the collecting together of huge multiplicities of atoms, so, according to Leibniz, they result from the aggregation of infinities of monads.[3] But how do monads unite into aggregates? The answer is that, in general, they do not *unite* at all. There are two types of monadic aggregates, "mere aggregates" and "real unities," and most aggregates found in nature are of the *mere* variety.

Given Leibniz' insistence that the only metaphysical realities are monads and their perceptions, it must be asked if the unity of a monadic aggregate—which alone underwrites its reality as a genuine "thing"—is purely perceptual, wholly a matter of appearing for others, or if it has some objective basis. The answer is neither yes nor no.

Consider our everday conception of a physical object. Why do we regard a drop of water, a grain of sand, or a tree as individual things, but not a cloud or a heap of sand or a stand of trees? Doubtless primarily because the former have a sort of "causal unity" the latter lack: when one part of a stone is turned, the other parts turn; when part of a tree is burned, the remainder is affected;

when part of a pebble is scratched, the vibrations are transmitted through the rest. The causal unity of a drop of water is relatively well-defined; when, for example, pressure is applied to one part, the others are deformed. A cloud, however, lacks such integrity; the particles of water that are its parts do not have a sufficiently close causal interrelationship—its unity as *one individual thing* lies wholly in the eyes of the beholder. This line of thought was espoused by Leibniz with respect to the unity of monadic aggregates, albeit with one important difference: the characteristically Leibnizian substitution of *perceptual* for *causal* unity.

There are clearly two ways in which a collection of monads can become aggregated into a single, specifiable thing, either (merely) *externally* united in being perceived as one thing by an external observing monad (so that we have not a genuine union, but a union for someone), or *internally* and genuinely united by the mutual perceptions of the component monads. The former mode of unity is that of the water particles that make up a cloud; the latter is that of the grains of stone that make up a single rock. Moreover, there may in certain cases be not merely an extensive interlinkage of mutually clear perceptions, as with the monads making up a certain rock or plank of wood, but a highly structured network of clear reciprocal perceptions among the monads making up a complexly articulated organism, as a plant or animal. Accordingly, four major possibilities must be discriminated with respect to aggregative configurations, in that the thing that is the object of perception may be:[4]

1. A simple *delusion* (e.g., a mirage).
2. A *disjointed* (or *mere*) *aggregate* whose sole being as one thing is being perceived as such (e.g., a herd of animals, a cloud of water droplets).
3. A *unified aggregate* (e.g., a stick or stone).
4. A *structured aggregate*; (e.g., a plant or animal).

A monadic aggregate is a single "individual thing" only in a figurative sense. Such "things" are not actually individual *things* at all—their unity is not firm enough for individuation. The aggregate *appears* as one, as a unit, and is thus a phenomenon by virtue of some genuine interrelationships among its constituents, a feature which gives it some footing in the real, monadic world, and makes it a well founded phenomenon.[5] But all such aggregates differ from real unities (such as human beings), in that they do not meet, or come close to meeting, the requirement of the principle of individuation—that of being single substances or at least coming close to them "in all practical purposes." The individuality of an aggregate is really "mental," i.e., perceptual: being realized only for internal or external observers, such monadic aggregates are mental entities (*entia mentalia*) which, having a genuine foundation in the monadic realm, are not (like a mirage) simply illusory or delusory phenomena, but *phaenomena bene fundata*.[6]

Leibniz' metaphysic thus does have a place for composites whose unity is more than *merely* phenomenal. In his view, the natural realm does comprise real things whose unity is intrinsic and actual, rather than a mere matter of appearance to external observers, (Contrast 4 above with 2).

3. *Causality and Action*

Causality is among the most basic well founded phenomena in the metaphysical system of Leibniz. Since each monad is separately "programmed" for the whole of its history, there is no such thing as causal interaction; the only interaction between monads arises in the reciprocal "perception" built into their mutual accord by pre-established harmony. The only thing monads can "do" in relation to one another is to perceive, and to agree (more or less) in their successive states; all talk of causal interaction is purely metaphorical.[7] In the system of Leibniz, causality is definable strictly in terms of monadic perception—when two monads come to have a state of agreement, that one in whose state this accord is inscribed more sharply, i.e., whose perceptions of the common transaction are clearer, is the active one, and the other the passive one in a strictly figurative "causal interaction." Leibniz writes:

> Thus action (or: *activity*) is to be attributed to a monad insofar as it has distinct perceptions, and passivity insofar as its perceptions are confused.[8]

In the correspondence with Arnauld this conception was developed in greater detail:

> This independence however does not prevent the inter-activity of substances among themselves, for, as all created substances are a continual production of the same sovereign Being according to the same designs and express the same universe or the same phenomena, they agree with one another exactly; and this enables us to say that one acts upon another because the one expresses more distinctly than the other the cause or reason for the changes,—somewhat as we attribute motion rather to a ship than to the whole sea; and this with reason, although, if we should speak abstractly, another hypothesis of motion could be maintained, that is to say, the motion in itself and abstracted from the

cause could be considered as something relative. It is thus, it seems to me, that the inter-activities of created substances among themselves must be understood. ...[9]

It is solely in terms of clearness of perception that efficient causation, itself a phenomenon rather than a monadic reality, comes to be well founded in the monadic realm.

4. Force and Matter

Materiality in the ordinary sense of the term has no place in Leibniz' conception of the monad. A single Leibnizian monad is no more material than a single Newtonian atom is colored. All material characteristics of the macro-objects of our everyday world are monadically *derivative*—secondary qualities rather than primary (in Locke's sense of these terms). They are wholly dependent on there being conglomerations of ultimate units.

Some important Leibnizian terms must be introduced in this connection. A characteristic is *primitive* if it characterizes monads, and *derivative* if it characterizes monadic aggregates, that is, if it derives in the aggregation of monads from some primitive monadic characteristic.[10] But what is primitive is simply the series of the states or perceptions of monads and nothing else. Thus Leibniz comes to call perception *primitive force*, the clear perceptions of a monad and its appetition toward new clear perceptions being its *primitive active force* (*vis primitiva agendi*) and its confused perceptions *primitive passive force* (*vis primitiva patiendi*) or, preferably, *prime matter* (materia prima).[11] As is typical of Leibniz, force and matter are correlative with the active principle (activity, agency, force) playing the fundamental role.

As can be expected, these primitive features of monads give rise to derivative aggregational characteristics. From the passive aspect of monads, their prime matter, there arises in aggregation what Leibniz calls "secondary matter" (*materia secunda*)—the "matter" of the physics of his time—along with its principal features, especially the two basic derivative passive forces (*vires derivativae patiendi*): inertia (*resistentia*) and solidity (impenetrability, *antitypia*).[12] There are also several derivative active forces (*vires a derivativae agendi*), the "forces" of the physics of the time, including especially what Leibniz terms "live force" (*vis viva*), by which he understands essentially what is now called kinetic energy,[13] and also *conatus* (or *solicitatio*, i.e., "virtual velocity"), whose ultimate foundation lies in monadic appetition. Thus Leibniz holds that the entire subject matter of the physical science of his time (terrestrial and celestial mechanics) is derived from the two primitive forces, since the structure of the monad, its series of perceptions, suffices to account for the fundamental concepts of mechanics.[14]

Leibniz mechanism enables him to proceed beyond this point, for according to it, all natural processes are complexes of mechanical ones, and thus all natural phenomena (animate perception alone excepted) can be explained mechanically. "It is the case that all the phenomena of material objects (*corpora naturalia*), excepting perceptions, can be accounted for in terms of magnitude, shape, and motion."[15] "All the phenomena of material objects (*corps*) can be explained mechanically or by the corpuscular philosophy, in accordance with certain mechanical principles. ...."[16] "Moreover in the phenomena, i.e., in the aggregate(s) resulting (from monads), all is explained mechanically. ...."[17] "Nature must always be explained mechanically and mathematically, provided one bears in mind that the principles or laws of mechanics themselves do not derive from mere mathematical extension, but from metaphysical reasons."[18] The mechanical properties of material objects are "derived" directly in aggregation, and their remaining properties are to be accounted for mechanically.

The fundamentality of force and the phenomenality of extension are key aspects of Leibniz' theory of matter. The whole tendency of his approach here puts him into diametric opposition to the Cartesian theory as matter as *res extensa*.

From this viewpoint we also see the intimate connection among Leibniz' metaphysic, his monadism, and his mechanistic position in natural philosophy. By making the derivation of mechanical characteristics suffice for aggregational characteristics in general, Leibniz' mechanism provides the machinery with which he endeavors to show the explanatory adequacy of the monadic theory.[19]

5. Harmony and Well Founding

What element is there in the structure of the realm of monads that makes it possible for well founded phenomena to arise? Any answer to this question must be provided by the pre-established harmony, which is responsible for any general, inter-monadic structure possessed by the realm of strictly independent monads.

We recall that an aggregate of monads is a (phenomenal) unit as a result of the duly correlated perceptions of monads;[20] thus phenomena arise in monadic perception.[21] Consequently there are two aspects to a well founded phenomenon, subjective and objective. The subjective aspects is brought to light in considering the perceiving monads themselves: the phenomenon is a unit since it is an *ens mentalis* for its perceiver. There is also an objective aspect in well founded phenomena: what is perceived is some feature of an actual aggregation of monads constituting a ground for perception because of certain similarities of state of its constituent monads. The well foundedness is thus the objective and the phenomenality the subjective side of the well founded phenomenon. Both of these states of affairs—the inner accord of the constituents of the aggregate, and the external accord of aggregate with percipient—prevail in virtue of the pre-established harmony. It is thus clear how the pre-established harmony, by providing the machinery for well founding, furnishes the key to the answer to our initial question in regard to the system of Leibniz.

These considerations indicate the ultimate reliance of Leibniz' theory of well founding on the Principle of Perfection. The connection between them is evidenced by the fact that the principle of well founding represents a facet of systemic economy, of complexity-minimization. Well founding is an aspect of perfection because it calls for economy in the machinery of cosmological explanation, holding that the phenomena are *in toto* to be accounted for by means of the metaphysical apparatus of monadological theory of substance.

NOTES

1. Cf. *Phil.*, II, p. 435.
2. See especially the essay *De modo distinguendi phaenomena realia ab imaginariis* (*Phil.*, VII, pp. 319-22; Loemker, pp. 363–6) to which we shall return in Chapter XII. It is important to realize that the various criteria Leibniz lays down here for the recognition of phenomena as real (well founded), e.g., their vividness and their congruity with the generally observed course of things, represent signs or marks of well foundedness, not its essence. The fact that these marks that are purely "internal" to the realm of observation attach to phenomena that are also well founded in the objective, monadic realm, turns on the pre-established harmony and the fact that this is the best of possible worlds. In effect we are thrown back upon the Cartesian concept that "God is no deceiver."
3. Leibniz himself draws this analogy between his own position and that of the atomists (*Phil.*, II, p. 252; Loemker, p. 531).
4. For Leibniz' own, more detailed scheme see the tabulation given in *Phil.*, II, p. 506.
5. Unlike a mere phenomenon which exists *only* in the "perceptions" of the observer without a corresponding foundation within the external realm of other

monads. In Leibniz, the real vs. illusory distinction is still preserved by distinguishing between well and ill founded phenomena.

6. The *things* of the sensible world are not the only *phaenomena bene fundata*; they are joined in this category by the perceptual space and time in which they are imbedded, as well as by the "causal" processes by which they seemingly interact.

7. In speaking of "causal interaction" we of course have in mind efficient causality. *Final* causality is another matter altogether; we shall return to it below.

8. *Monadology*, §49. Cf. *Phil.*, II, pp. 57, 59, 71, 112, 113; and VII, p. 312.

9. *Phil.*, II, p. 147. Leibniz utilizes this concept of activity also in the context of voluntary human action: "... our voluntary action, however, is always spontaneous, in such a way that its principle is in the agent" (*Causa Dei*, §28; *Phil.*, VI, p. 443).

10. *Phil.*, pp. 251, 306, 517; *Math.*, VI, pp. 101, 236.

11. *Phil.*, II, pp. 206, 244, 245, 250, 251, 252; *Math.*, VI, pp. 100–1.

12. *Phil.*, II, pp. 171, 184, 306; *Math.*, VI, pp. 100, 236–7.

13. Its derivtive character is assured by the statement: "The forces which arise from mass and velocity are derivative" (*Phil.*, II, p. 251; Loemker, p. 530). Regarding derivative active forces see also *Phil.*, II, pp. 2, 171, 201ff., 275–6, and *Math.*, VI, pp. 101–3 and 236–7.

14. For Leibniz' derivation of mechanics see the essay *Specimen dynamicum pro admirandis naturae legibus circa corporum vires et mutuas actiones detegendis et ad suas causas revocandis* (*Math.*, VI, pp. 234 ff., cf. pp. 98 ff.).

15. *Phil.*, II, p. 314.

16. *Ibid.*, p. 78.

17. *Ibid.*, p. 250 (Loemker, p. 528). This holds good even in the organic realm, for even organic things are a kind of automation or natural machine, "which is a machine not only as whole, but also in the smallest parts" (PNG, §3; *Monadology*, §64).

18. *Phil.*, II, p. 58 (Loemker, p. 338).

19. This aspect of Leibniz' mechanism is most explicit in his illuminating letter to de Volder (*Phil.*, II, pp. 248–53; Loemker, pp. 528–31).

20. "... only monads will be real, but the union will be supplied in the phenomenon by the action (*operatio*) of the perceiving soul" (*Phil.*, II, p. 435; Loemker, p. 600.

21. "The explanation of all phenomena proceeds solely through the perceptions of monads functioning in harmony with each other. ..." (*Phil.*, II, p. 450; Loemker, p. 604). See also the *Système Nouveau* (*Phil.*, IV, pp. 471–77). The pre-established harmony was termed "the hypothesis of the concomitance or of the accord of substances between themselves" in the correspondence with Arnauld, a far more suggestive terminology. (*Phil.*, II, pp. 58, 74, etc.)

Chapter X

Space and Time: Motion and Infinity

1. *The Basis of Leibniz' Theory of Space and Time*

Leibniz advocated a theory of space (and time) as "relative"—that is, as relative to the things ordinarily said to be located *within* space (or time). He opposed the doctrine of Newton's *Principia* which cast space and time in the role of containers existing in their own right, and having a make-up that is altogether indifferent to the things emplaced in them. Owing to the general tenor of his theory Leibniz is sometimes seen as a precursor of Einstein and modern relativity theory. But this view is mistaken or, at any rate, misleading. For Leibniz—unlike Einstein and the modern relativists—is not thinking of the relativity of dynamical principles to the choice of a coordinate system *within* nature, so that we compare the situation from the perspective of various world-included coordinate-frameworks. Rather, Leibniz's thesis that "space is relative to the things in it" relates to the perspective of various alternative possible worlds taken as a whole.

To put the matter somewhat generally, one can say that the core of Leibniz' theory of space and time is that these are nothing apart from the things "in" them, but owe their existence and indeed their very nature to the ordering relations that obtain among things.[1] Space and time are thus not receptacles which exist independently of and (logically) prior to the existence of the entities which are supposedly embedded within them. They are (well founded) *phenomena*, and as such their existence is secondary, since it is derivative from the substances (and their properties) which they "contain."

The general character of the process of derivation that Leibniz envisages for space and time is readily pictured. In regard to space, all monads perceive one another at every given temporal juncture, so the entire actual world is (for each of its member monads) one vast monadic aggregate at any given time. For Leibniz, space is this relationship among all the monads inherent in their contemporaneous mutual perceptions, their general universal ordering throughout time (i.e., at any given time). The general order obtaining among the monads of this world in virtue of the pre-established harmony, and thus resting ultimately on the

Principle of Perfection, is the basis for the well founding of the phenomenon of space.

The situation is similar with respect to time. The mutual agreement obtaining between monadic states in virtue of the pre-established harmony is such that, to every state of a given monad at some instant of its private time, there corresponds exactly one (contemporaneous) state of every other monad. This correspondence is defined in terms of closeness of similarity. (It might be helpful to draw an analogy with two skew lines in space—to every point on each there corresponds just one point of the other that lies nearest to it.) It is this corresponding state of the other monad, the state most similar to it on the basis of *purely qualitative* comparisons, that is simultaneous (contemporaneous) with it in public, intermonadic time. Time as well as space is derivative from the primitive characteristics of the individual monads.

The fact that our actual universe has its particular kind of spatial and temporal structure is, for Leibniz, a contingent feature of this world. If an imperfect deity has created an imperfect world, one in which the mutual perceptions of the (independent) monads did not accord neatly, the world might have had a very different sort of spatial structure—perhaps non-continuous one. Similarly, if the appetitions of the independent monadic programs did not exhibit the requisite matching and coherence, time (i.e., public, inter-monadic time, in contrast to the private time built into each individual monadic program) would not have anything like the "equable flow" envisaged by Newton.

2. *The Nature of Space and Time*

The universal correspondence established by the mutual attunement of all created individual substances is the result, not of any sort of causal influence, but of the coordination of all substances comprising a common world.[2] Each substance, however, by no means is represented or perceived by every other substance in an equally sharp and detailed way; each one perceives more clearly those substances closer to, or more important for, it,[3] perceiving the whole universe from its own point of view. Leibniz compares the individual monad to

> a center or point which, though itself simple, is the locus of an infinity of angles formed by the lines which intersect at it.[4]

This mutual coordination of monads is the foundation for space and time. Apart from the concordance of the mutual perceptions of monads, spatial relationships have no place in the monadic realm: "there is no spatial or absolute distance or propinquity of monads, and to say that they are compressed in a point, or disseminated in space, is to make use of certain fictions of our spirit."[5]

Against Leibniz' theory of space as a well founded phenomenon, Russell objects[6] that Leibniz cannot regard space as purely phenomenal and subjective because, as he puts it, "the perceptions of different monads differ [objectively], owing to the difference of their points of view." The objection, though correct, is not damaging to Leibniz, and not wholly fair to him. The essentials of his position are clear: the monads and their states (perceptions) are basic. These perceptions are coordinated (in the pre-established harmony) to give rise to a system of mutually accommodating points of view. Space as a well founded phenomenon results from this system of coordinated perceptions.

At no two different moments of time can an individual substance have the same state, for if its state were exactly the same, the whole system of its contemporary substance states would have to be the same, and therefore, moments of time being defined in terms of contemporary substance states, the moments of time would also be the same. Thus each individual substance is subject to a perpetual, continuous change of state, the only activity of which it is capable.[7] Leibniz chooses to call it appetition but connotations of this term toward some sort of active, conscious, seeking or striving must be avoided.

From the very first, Leibniz presented the monad as a *continuant*, a perduring substance persisting through change;[8] in mathematical jargon a one-parameter family of states is involved,[9] the history of the monad being given by a continuous function characterizing its monadic states. This change of state of a substance (appetition) is temporally continuous, and at any instant every monad represents the entire universe from its own point of view with varying degrees of clarity,[10] making for the continuous distribution of monads in space. Space, like time, is a structure of relations of an appropriate sort.

Time, for Leibniz, is conceptually coordinate with space: one could not have space in an atemporal context, not conversely. For space is the order of *co-existence*—that is, the order among the mutually contemporaneous status of things; while time is the order of *succession*—that is, the order among the various different mutually coexisting states of things which—*qua* mutually coexisting—must, of course, have some sort of "spatial" structure.

It is helpful to clarify what is going on here by means of pictorial cinematographic analogy. (To be sure, Leibniz himself did not think of the matter in this naive pictorial way. But he thought of it in roughly equivalent terms—namely, in terms of mathematical analogues in the theory of real-variable functions.) Take a motion picture film: the film reels, say, for "Gone With The Wind." And let suppose that an immense jig-saw puzzle is created by the cutting up of this film—first into individual frames and then even more finely. The Leibnizian ordering problem is now a two-fold one, first to assemble all of the individual frames—the contemporaneity (or coexistence) slices that define its spatial order; and secondly the ordering of these contemporaneity slices into proper sequence that defines a temporal order. For Leibniz, space and time thus stand in an inseparable co-ordination with one another within the overall ordering process that leads from the starting point of the particular states of individual substances and arrives at an all-comprehending spatio-temporal order. This coordinated symbiosis of space and time is an important aspect of Leibniz's metaphysics. For him—unlike Kant—space and time are mutually coordinate in such a way that neither is more fundamental than the other.

Space, according to Leibniz, is an *ordering of coexisting things*, but what are the *things* at issue? Two alternative answers, both perfectly proper, can be given. Taking the "things" at issue here as monads, we arrive at metaphysical space; taking them as aggregates, as phenomena, we arrive at the perceived space with which one deals in ordinary life and in the sciences. Both, of course, are ultimately phenomenal—space is never a substance, a thing in its own right.

To illustrate the nature of space as a system of order, Leibniz uses as example the relationships of a family tree,"[11] and also adduces another example of order or relation which, although it is somewhat lengthly, merits consideration *in extenso* because it throws much light on the logical foundations of Leibniz' philosophy:

> The ratio or proportion between two lines L and M, may be conceived three several ways; as a ratio of the greater L, to the lesser M; as a ratio of the lesser M, to the greater L; and lastly, as something abstracted from both, that is, as the ratio between L and M, without considering which is the antecedent, or which the consequent; which the subject, and

which the object. And thus it is, that proportions are considered in music. In the first way of considering them, L the greater; in the second, M the lesser, is the subject of that accident, which philosophers call relation. But, which of them will be the subject, in the third way of considering them? It cannot be said that both of them, L and M together, are the subject of such an accident;[12] for if so, we should have an accident in two subjects, with one leg in one, and the other in the other; which is contrary to the notion of accidents. Therefore we must say, that this relation, in this third way of considering it, is indeed out of the subjects; but being neither a substance, nor an accident, it must be a mere ideal thing, the consideration of which is nevertheless useful.[13]

Here the basis of Leibniz' denial of reality to space and time is brought fully to light. They are relational and *eo ipso* incapable of qualifying as *things* in their own right.

Time, too, has a dual nature for Leibniz. There is the essentially private, intra-monadic time of each individual substance continuing, by appetition, through its transitions from state to state. There is also the public time obtaining throughout the system of monads in general, made possible by the inter-monadic correlations established by the pre-established harmony. Leibniz' standard definition of time as *the order of non-contemporaneous things*[14] would be vitiated by an obvious circularity if it did not embody a distinction between intra- and inter-monadic time, carrying the latter back to (i.e., well founding it within) the former.

The monads are ordered continuously in their point of view; it is always possible to find a monad differing from a given monad in point of view by less than any preassigned difference. This is basic to both the Leibnizian theory of space and to his denial of a vacuum in nature. The monads are also continuously ordered with regard to structure. As Russell puts it, "If two substances differ by a finite difference there must be ... a continuous series of intermediate substances, each of which differs infinitesimally from the next."[15]

It follows from these considerations concerning the optimality of the realm of monads that physical space is a plenum.[16] Moreover, all the processes of the physical world, e.g., motion or impact, take place continuously, according to Leibniz.[17] The principle of continuity as applied to the physical world, Leibniz' extension of the classical principle *natura non facit saltus*, is put to work by him throughout the physical and metaphysical domains.

3. *Space and Time: Some Polemical Issues*

Leibniz' central argument against the independent reality of space and time is that this would violate the Principle of Sufficient Reason. The following is a good formulation of this argument:

> Space is something absolutely uniform; and, without the things placed in it, one point of space does not absolutely differ in any respect whatsoever from another point of space. Now from hence it follows, (supposing space to be something in itself, besides the order of bodies among themselves,) that 'tis impossible there should be a reason, why God, preserving the same situations of bodies among themselves, should have placed them in space after one certain particular manner, and not otherwise; why every thing was not placed the quite contrary way, for instance, by changing East into West[18]

Absolute time would similarly violate the Principle of Sufficient Reason, and is therefore impossible.[19] The independence of time would further violate the Principle of Perfection, for, if this were possible, God might have created the world sooner, thus increasing the amount of existence, and hence of perfection.[20]

These arguments are not soely intended to refute the absoluteness of space and time, but additionally to dispense with the substantiality of spatial extension as conceived of by the Cartesians. Leibniz held that the Cartesians erred in regarding spatiality as pertaining to substances, for he regarded extension not as something primitive, but as derived from substances. The concept of substance which gives rise to the monad is simply inapplicable to space. Leibniz also has an *argumentum ad hominem* against the Cartesian position. He argues that spatial extension is nothing privileged, and that if it gives rise to substance, so ought temporal extension.'[21]

There are three aspects of the theory of space of Newton, as defended by Clarke, which Leibniz is especially concerned to refute—the absoluteness of space, the existence of a void, and the thesis that space is the sensorium of God. Leibniz also wishes to refute the suggestion made by Clarke in his third letter that space is some sort of property.

Leibniz' refutation of absolute space, based on the argument that this invoves a violation of the Principle of Sufficient Reason, we have considered already. The impossibility of a void is shown by arguing that a void would be a special case of an absolute space:

> The same reason, which shows that extramundane space is imaginary, proves that all empty space is an imaginary thing; for they differ only as greater and less.[22]

The position that space is the sensorium of God is met by Leibniz on theological grounds, for if this were so, space would be an entity wholly outside of God's power, and He would be dependent upon it.[23]

Next we come to Leibniz' arguments against the thesis that space is a property or attribute. If this were true, it would have to belong to some substance, but then what of void space?[24] If space *is not* regarded as an attribute of God it would be completely beyond his power, and there would be an infinity of eternal things beside God;[25] if it *is* a property of God, "It does not appear reasonable to say, that this empty space, either round or square, is a property of God."[26] Further, "a property of God must (which is very strange) be made up of the affections of creatures; for all finite spaces, taken together, make up infinite space."[27] If space is regarded as a property of the things which occupy it, then the distinction between space and place breaks down[28] and so Leibniz feels that he has completely disposed of the thesis that space is a property.

So far we have dealt almost solely with the negative and polemical portions of Leibniz' theory of space and time. Let us now consider the positive part of that theory. As indicated already, Leibniz oft-stated position is that space and time are orders of things, and not things.

In his fifth letter to Clarke, Leibniz gives his answer to the psychological questions of the origin of the notion of space.[29] It is essentially that the *place* of an object is its relation to a number of other objects whose relations to each other are not changed, and *space* is "that which results from all places taken together."[30] This ordering of positions relates not *abstracta* but *substances*:

> Now simple substance, although it does not in itself have extension, nevertheless has position, which is the ground of extension, since extension is the continuous simultaneous repetition of position—as we say a line is made by the fluxion of a point. ...[31]

Space and time are ideal, or rather are phenomena,[32] space because it is nothing but the order or relation of (simultaneous) existents, and time since it is relational, and involves the labyrinth of the continuum.[33] However, space and time are not chimera but well founded phenomena, *phaenomena bene fundata*. There arises the question of what monadic properties and characteristics provide the *fundamenta* for space and time.

Let us first consider space. How is the difference in relation or position grounded within the monad? In the internal composition of every monad is reflected its relations to all others. We are once more brought back to the pre-established harmony, which sees to it that each monad mirrors the universe from its own point of view. This alone is the *fundamentum* of space. Time is grounded in the change of state, the appetition, of the monads, for Leibniz defines temporal order in terms of monadic states:

> If of two elements which are not simultaneous one comprehends the ground (*ratio*) of the other the former is considered as preceding, the latter as succeeding.[34]

The space and time we have been considering are those to which the monads, the actual substances, belong; this space and time are manifolds of order among the monads with respect to coexistence and succession, respectively.[35] This is the fashion in which space and time are conceived of in the correspondence with Clarke. However, at times, Leibniz has in mind not the actual space/time framework of *this* world, but space/time frameworks in general—including those matrices of order established with respect to other possible worlds. (More of this anon.)

Some further aspects of Leibniz' theory of space and time deserve mention:

1. *The Dimensionality of Space.* Leibniz defends a position which at first seems inconsistent with other parts of his theory of space. He holds that tri-dimensionality of space is *necessary*, even though space itself is but the order of contingents. To Clarke he objects that absolute space is a limitation on God, and yet insists on the absoluteness of its dimensions.

> But with the dimensions of matter it is not thus: the ternary number is determined for it not by the reason of the best, but by a geometrical necessity, because the geometricians have been able to prove that there are only three straight lines perpendicular to one another which can intersect at one and the same point.[36] Nothing more appropriate could have been chosen to show the difference there is between the moral necessity that accounts for the choice of wisdom and the brute necessity of Strato and the adherents of Spinoza, who deny to God understanding and will, than a consideration of the difference existing between the reason for the laws of motion and the reason for the ternary number of the dimensions: for the first lies in the choice of the best and the second in a geometrical and blind necessity.[37]

However, the reasons motivating Leibniz to take this position are brought to light in the correspondence with Clarke.[38] The dimensionality of space must be determined by an absolute necessity, for if more dimensions had been possible, God could have created a somehow "bigger" universe.

2. *The Measurability of Space and Time.* To Clarke's objection, "that Space and Time are quantities, which Situation and Order are not,"[39] Leibniz replies:

> Relative things have their quantity, as well as absolute ones. For instance, ratios or proportions in mathematics, have their quantity, and are measured by logarithms; and yet they are relations. And therefore though time and space consist in relations, yet they have their quantity.[40]

The amount of time between two moments is an exact measure of the number or volume of intermediary states of the universe. Into a given amount of time only a certain fixed number of distinct states of the universe can be put, neither more nor less. The amount of time is an exact measure of temporal order, and this can only be altered by adding or dropping some states which, with the actual state of affairs, is impossible.[41] This gets Leibniz around the difficulty that an order-preserving one-one correspondence is possible between line-segments of different lengths.[42] The measurability of both spatial and temporal relations rests on the fact that:

> In both these orders—time and space—we can speak of *propinquity* or *remoteness* of the elements according as *fewer or more connecting links are required to discern their mutual order.* Two points, then, are nearer to one another when the points between them and the structure arising out of them with maximal definiteness, present something relatively simpler.[43]

It is interesting to note that in a passage of the *Nouveaux Essais* Leibniz asserts the possibility of a changeless duration, an "empty" time.[44] In this respect time is unlike space in which no void is possible. A void in space would be measurable, but a void in time would be of indeterminate length, and whoever maintained that it was of length zero, i.e., had no duration at all, could not be refuted.[45] Thus a "durée sans changemens" is possible because its actualization would make no difference. However, arguing strictly from the Principle of the Identity of Indiscernibles, Leibniz ought to have taken a more positive stand. He should have maintained that a temporal vacuum is just as impossible as a spatial one.

3. *Space and Analysis Situs.* Against Leibniz' theory of space the objection of strangeness may be brought, though perhaps by now it is sufficiently clear that such an objection is valid neither in science nor in philosophy. Leibniz' space is a space of real points (i.e., monads) without real lines, planes, or solids; it is a space where one can tell—if one is God—whether two monad-points are

close together (for then their points of view will be similar), and yet it is meaningless to ask for the distance between them, for distance, being a relation, has no place in the monadic realm.

Such a world must have seemed weird a century ago, but these spaces, termed *topological* spaces, are the common familiar property of mathematicians today. Topology is a branch of mathematics that has received much attention of late. In the last century it was called *analysis situs;* fittingly enough, its founder was Leibniz.[46]

4. *The Non-Homogeneity of Time.* There is a total lack of homogeneity in time, according to Leibniz. He holds that it is not only impossible that the state of the universe is the same at two different instants, but even that every earlier state of the universe has a logical, or natural, priority over every later state.[47] Precisely what it is that Leibniz has in mind one can only conjecture. I should suggest that this priority is a consequence of continuity considerations. An earlier instant cannot be interchanged with a later one because this would involve a break in the continuity of the development of the universe.

4. *The Plurality of Space-Time Frameworks*

As Leibniz saw it, the Newtonian theory of "absolute" space maintained space as an entity in its own right, a content-neutral container which would be filled up with different substantive content in the case of different possible worlds. His own theory holds that space is itself something content-relative. It derives the view of the Newtonians that Space, like God, is unique and in principle compatible with various different world-orders, and implies—by way of contrast—that every possible world must have its own characteristic spatial structure.[48] The issue comes down to a *metaphysical*—rather than *physical*—bone of contention. For in physics we necessarily study *this* world alone, while the point at issue is that of the question: Do *different* "possible worlds" have their own spatial structure or should they be conceptualized as different ways of felling up one single common content-indifferent spaced-time container?

To begin with, it must be recognized that the *idea or conception* of space will (for Leibniz) be uniformly one and the same with respect to all possible worlds. This is true for space as it is for any and every *concept.* The *concept* of spatiality is world-uniform because it is world-indifferent. A possible world may or may not contain *men*, and its intelligent creatures may be very different from ours, but it cannot alter what *humanity* is. (The concept of humanity may not find *application* in some other possible world, but it cannot undergo *alteration* there.) In every world-setting space answers to the same conception—it is "the order of *coexistence*" (not—be it noted—the order of coexistents, which, after all, will differ from world to world). For Leibniz, every concept is what it is with respect to any and every possible world—the concept of space included.

A space for Leibniz is an order of *coexisting* substances, and distinct individuals in distinct worlds do not coexist with one another. (*Coexisting* substances are *a fortiori compossible*.) There were as many such orders as there are families of *compossibilia*. The limits of a space are coordinate with the realm of the substances comprising its correlative world.

If Leibniz had defined space as the order of possible existents at large—rather than as the order of possible *co*-existents—then, to be sure, there would only be one single, all-comprehending superspace.[49] For it is clear that different substances in different possible worlds do bear various relations to one another—the relation of *difference* for one thing, but also *sameness of attribute* (in various regards) and so on. But while there are cross-world *relations* among possible substances, there are not (as I interpret Leibniz) any cross-world *spatial relations*. Space is the order of *co*-existence, and spatial relations are confined to coexistents.

Leibniz holds that every possible world has its own space as it has its own laws. There are *many* spaces, even as there are many law-manifolds:

> ... there could exist an infinity of other spaces and worlds entirely different [from ours]. They would have no distance from us [nor other special relations to us] if the spirits inhabiting them had sensations not related to ours. Exactly as the world and the space of dreams differ from our waking world, there could even be in such a world quite different laws of motion.[50]

Distinct worlds are spatially disjoint—or better (since disjointness is itself a spatial term) they are spatially *unrelated* disjoint not only in a *physical* but even in an *intellectual* sense—somewhat like the dream-worlds of different people. The spaces here discussed, which exist independently of the actual world, exist only in the mind of God, since this is where the possible worlds have their being.[51] In the extremely interesting opuscule "On Existence, Dreams, and Space," Leibniz writes:

[S]pace [is] that which makes that many perceptions cohere with each other at the same time. ... The idea of space is, therefore, that through which, as is recognized, we separate clearly the place, and even the world, of dreams, from ours. ... From this it follows furthermore that there can be infinitely many spaces and, hence, worlds, such that between them and ours there is to be no distance. Plainly as the world and space of dreams differ from ours, so too can they have other laws of motion. ... When we awake from dreams we come upon more congruences that govern bodies, but not that govern minds. Whoever asks whether another world, or another space, can exist is asking to this extent whether there are minds that can communicate nothing to us.[52]

With Leibniz, moreoever, there is a special reason why there can be no such thing as a many-world embracing superspace. He held that, for Leibniz, a substance internalizes its relations to others in the property-system that constitutes its complete individual notions. Insofar as they go beyond this property-internalization, all relations are only "things of the mind," mere *entia rationis* whose "being" is virtual and imaginary, devoid of any real existence in its own right.[53] The spatial relations among substances of the same possible world—like all other relations among them—thus have at least a derivative possibility of reality, namely that which arises through the prospect of their being realized along with their terms. But a "relationship" among the incompatible substances of different possible worlds—since they relate *incompossible* terms—can never have both feet together on at least the *terra infirma* of possible realization. It is, for Leibniz, already stretching matters to speak of spatial relations among compossibilities; to contemplate spatial relations among *incompossibles* would stretch the concept of spacial relatedness beyond its working limits. (As we have seen, space is "the order of *existence*," and incompossible being such that—by their very nature—they cannot possibly coexist.)

But even if distinct worlds have distinct spaces, will it not nevertheless be the case that the spatial *structure* of other worlds will be the same—or at any rate similar—to the spatial structure of ours?

There is nothing in Leibniz's philosophy that constrains him to answer this leading question affirmatively. Consider the possible world whose Eiffel Tower was built a bit shorter (say because the iron founders who made the girders worked a trifle less exactly). Its substances are in general so similar to those of our world that its spatial structure would be virtually identical with that of ours.

But this is a very specialized circumstance, one that will certainly not be realized in general.

In thinking of the manifold of Leibnizian possible worlds we must avoid any inclination to keep our imagination under too tight a rein. Possible worlds can differ from ours very drastically indeed. And worlds whose substances are radically different and behave in line with radically different laws of nature might well have a spatial structure quite different from ours. Indeed Leibniz' project of *analysis situs* ("topology" as we nowadays call it) actually represents an attempt to devise a theory of spatial relationships which does not involve the whole range of specific commitments of a full-blown Euclidean geometry. (Leibniz would not have been surprised at the discovery of non-Euclidean geometries, and that he would have had no difficulty in assimilating them to his theory of space.)

We come finally to a rather delicate Leibnizian issue. Could a possible world lack having a spatiotemporal structure altogether? Could the states of its substances be in such a whirl of "blooming, buzzing confusion" that a space-time order is lacking altogether?

Presumably not. After all, even a chaotic arrangement is some sort of "ordering"—even a random ordering is an ordering (and a very characteristic sort of ordering at that). To be sure, there are possible worlds so chaotic in their make-up that it would be inappropriate to characterize the relationships among the states of its substances as generating a "spatiotemporal order" *as we know it*, judging in terms of the continuities and regularities of our world. But to say this is to say little more than that the world with which we are familir—the world we ourselves inhabit—is a very special one in the Leibnizian framework. It is, after all, the best possible world in a respect that puts prime emphasis on lawfulness and rational order.

5. *A Difficulty Regarding Time*

At any point of time there must clearly be *something* to differentiate the then-actual state of a substance from its other (equally real but nonconcurrent) states: some sort of light to illuminate the then-given frame, to revert to a cinematographic analogy. The logic of the situation is such that Leibniz' metaphysical machinery of an atemporal God and transtemporal individual concepts needs to be supplemented by some specifically temporal device for chronology-generation. Not only does Leibniz fail to provide such a device, but he entertains a variety of metaphysical commitments of an entirely static and timeless character which make it dubious that any such device can be provided in his system without generating internal stresses of intolerable proportions. The difficulty here goes to the very root of Leibniz' dynamism. How to extract change from the changeless? The puzzle is the ancient one to which Zeno of Elea had already put his hand: How is one to provide a rationalization of process within the framework of a metaphysic whose stance is fundamentally static and atemporal—like the system of Leibniz tends to be, by virtue of the fact that everything that occurs in the world's history is mapped out in God's mind *sub ratione possibilitatis* prior to the creation. The deo-centric metaphysic of Leibniz can take us as far as the *concepts* of change, activity, and process. The things for which these concepts stand are of problematic access. Ironically for a philosopher who put action, activity, and dynamism at the center of his metaphysic, the status of the transient *now* that is so crucial to the issue of temporal process remains a mystery.

6. *Motion*

In the dialogue *Pacidus Philalethi* of 1676, in which various of the major doctrines of Leibniz' later philosophy are adumbrated, he adheres to an interesting theory of motion, that of transcreation.[54] He writes that motion

> cannot, I think, be better explained than when we say that the body E is somehow extinguished and annihilated in place B and actually created anew and resuscitated in placed D, which can be called, in new and most happy terminology, *transcreation*.[55]

This involves the continuous miracle which Leibniz later often deplores in criticizing occasionalism, but which he regarded favorably at this early stage, saying that "genuine and authentic miracles happen daily in nature."[56]

When his philosophy had matured Leibniz rejected transcreation, for by then he had a solution to the physical continuum problem which the doctrine of transcreation was constructed to evade. Writing to de Volder in 1699, Leibniz says:

> I added the hypothesis of transcreation for the sake of illustration, speaking philosophically and particularly like the Cartesians, who say, with some ground, that God creates all things continuously. For them, therefore, moving a body is nothing but reproducing it in successively different places, and it would have to be shown that this reproduction cannot take place in leaps. Rather, this could not be shown without returning to the reason which I have proposed for the universal law of

continuity. ... However, this hypothesis of leaps cannot be refuted except by the principle of order, with the aid of the supreme reason, which does everything in the most perfect way.[57]

Let us now turn to Leibniz' mature theory of motion. In his *Dynamica,* motion is defined as characterizing those bodies whose points do not remain in the same place, i.e., motion is temporal change of place.[58] Leibniz must hold motion to be a phenomenon, for this is the case with both space and time. Witness the following passage:

... matter and motion ... are phenomena whose reality is rooted in the mutual perceptions of the things (at diverse times) and in the harmony with other perceptions.[59]

The phenomenality of motion is made necessary because, as we have seen, physical motion is *relative*:

Motion, in mathematincal rigor, is nothing other than the mutual change of position of bodies, nor is it anything somehow absolute, but consists in relation.[60]

This relational character of motion is alone sufficient, given Leibniz' intrinsic theory of relations, to relegate it to the realm of phenomena.

However, like all phenomena of the physical world, motion has its foundation in the monadic realm. For:

... if there is nothing to motion than this mutual change [of place], it follows that nothing in nature affords a reason (*ratio*) for its being necessary to ascribe the motion to one thing [of those moving relatively] rather than to another. The consequence of this would be that there is no such thing as real motion.[61]

Thus motion can be studied from the starting point of its *fundamentum* in the real world. From this metaphysical point of view it must be absolute, not relative. When in his fourth letter Clarke urges that motion is a "really different state," and holds that this is negated by any theory holding physical motion to be relative,[62] Leibniz grants the former assertion, but questions the latter, saying:

I reply that motion is independent of observation, but that it is not independent of observability.[63]

Leibniz holds that although motion in the physical world is indeed relative, it is absolute in the metaphysical world in virtue of its well founding, and so it is possible for God to tell which bodies are "really" in motion.[64]

However, I agree that there is a difference between an absolute and
genuine motion of a body and a motion simply relative to its position
with respect to another body. For when the immediate cause of a change
is in a body, it is genuinely in motion and then the position of the others
with regard to it will change as a consequence, although the cause of this
change does not reside at all in them.[65]

Thus, of a number of bodies in relative motion, only those are
"really" in motion in which the *actual cause* of the change (*cause
immédiate du changement* or *ratio mutationis*) resides.[66] Let us
examine more closely the nature of this cause of motion.

As early as the dialogue *Pacidus Philalethi* (1676) Leibniz had
maintained that whatever moves has a proper tendency to motion.[67]
This constitutes an adumbration of his later idea of a "solicitation
to motion," a tendency to motion constituted by an infinitesimal *vis
viva*.[68] Leibniz writes:

> ... that which is real and absolute in motion consists not in what is
> purely mathematical, such as change in neighbourhood or situation, but
> in motive force itself.[69]

Consequently the solicitation, like the *vis viva* itself, is derivative
from the activity of monads, and so the *fundamentum* of motion is
active primitive force. It is thanks to this well founding of motion
that God, in virtue of his knowledge of the monadic world, is able
to distinguish between true and merely relative motion.

Since no monad is without activity, it follows that no aggregate
is wholly without *vis viva*. Consequently no body can be totally at
rest:

> It is indeed true that, to speak exactly, there is no body whatever that is
> perfectly and entirely at rest, but this is something from which one
> abstracts in considering the matter mathematically.[70]

This accords beautifully with the principle of continuity. There is,
in metaphysical strictness, no bifurcation of the bodies of the
universe into those at rest and those in motion. Such a division is a
merely practical device.

7. *Infinity*

Not only was Leibniz concerned with continuity in philosophy
and natural science, but as a mathematician he was eager to dispel
the problems which arise in connection with it. The history of these
problems goes back to the arguments of Zeno against motion and
the many. The central issue can be put simple: How can a space or
time-filling *interval* consist of points which do not fill space or

instants which do not fill time? How can indivisibles constitute a continuum?

This problem Leibniz terms the *labyrinth* of the continuum and indivisibles.[71] Concerning it he writes:

> It is not possible to get a thread through the labyrinth concerning the composition of the continuum or concerning the greatest (maximum) and the least (minimum) and the unnamable and the infinite unless geometry gets it; in fact, no one arrives at a sound metaphysic except the man who comes over to it by that way.[72]

Leibniz did not dwell on the philosophic importance of this problem without having arrived at a solution to it that was satisfactory to himself. Before we can proceed to the study of this solution we must deal with *infinity*, another notion which is very important in Leibniz' thought.

Leibniz, on wholly logical grounds, rejects the notion of infinite number, holding that a definition must involve a proof of the possibility of the thing defined, as he had maintained earlier against Descartes' ontological proof.[73] It is this which invalidates the notion of infinite number in Leibniz' view.[74] He did, however, attempt some qualitative approaches to the classification of infinites. For example, he distinguishes in the correspondence with des Bosses between a categorematic infinity (which, he argues, cannot exist) and a syncategorematic and a supercategorematic infinity.

The denial of infinite number forces Leibniz to deal with two questions:

1. How, if infinitely large numbers are impossible, are the infinitesimals or infinitely small numbers demanded by the calculus possible?
2. How, if there is no infinite number, is an infinite variety of created things, or for that matter any of the infinities of the metaphysical world, possible?

The first question is on the whole consistently answered by a denial of infinitely small numbers. We find Leibniz writing to Bernouilli:

> For if we suppose that there actually exist the segments on the line that are to be designated by $\frac{1}{2}$, $\frac{1}{4}$ ..., and that all the members of this sequence actually exist, you conclude from this that an infinitely small member must also exist. In my opinion, however the assumption implies nothing but the existence of any finite fraction of arbitrary smallness.[75]

The second problem resulting from the denial of infinite number, that of the infinite variety of the monads and their properties, is dealt with by maintaining that here there is a variety too rich to be encompassed by any numerical bound.[76] Such an infinity is the only one admitted by Leibniz; he terms it an *actual infinity*. It surpasses all numerical bounds in content, and is immeasurable by an infinite number.

This actual infinity is the darling of nature, which affects it everywhere.[77] The actual infiniteness of the real, as opposed to the finiteness encountered in the world of physics, is not the source of a gulf between physics and metaphysics. It is rather, Leibniz feels, the source of a wonderful agreement embodied in his philosophy. Thus he writes:

> It is found (turns out) that the rules of the finite succeed in the infinite, as if there were atoms ... , and that vice versa the rules of the infinite succeed in the finite, as if there were infinitely small metaphysical [points].[78]

It is important for Leibniz to supply an answer to the question, How does an actual infinity avoid giving rise to infinite number, and thus lead to contradiction? The answer provides Leibniz with the saving thread for the continuum labyrinth. It proceeds from the remark that there are two ways of putting number to the variety of real things in the universe, and goes on to demonstrate that neither of these is legitimate.

(1) One might regard the whole universe as one unity, and try to discern the constituents which make it up, thus counting its parts (a procedure which, of course, only God could undertake). But this cannot be done, for:

> The true infinity, strictly speaking, is only in the absolute, which exists before all composition and is not at all formed by the addition of parts.[79]

The absolute whole can be divided, but not resolved into ultimate parts or constituents capable of enumeration, since there are certain kinds of wholes or unities which are logically prior to their parts, and therefore cannot be resolved into them. Leibniz gives the following example:

> Unity is divisible, but is not resolvable; for the fractions which are parts of unity have less simple notions, because integers (less simple than unity) always enter into the notions of fractions. Several people who have philosophized, in mathematics, about the point and unity, have become confused, for want of distinguishing between resolution into notions and division into parts. Parts are not always simpler than the whole, though they are always less than the whole.[80]

In accord with this argument, an actual whole, though divisible into actual parts, cannot be resolved into actual ultimate constituents, because the ultimate constituents are mere notions and have no reality.

(2) There is the complementary way of assigning number to an infinite collection by a consecutive exhaustion of the individuals constituting that collection, but in the case under consideration this is not possible. The only reals are monads, and the collections to be numbered aggregates; these aggregates, being phenomenal, lack the unity requisite for enumeration. As Russell puts it, the position of Leibniz is that "one whole must be one substance, and to what is not one whole number cannot properly be applied."[81] Or, in Leibniz' own words,

> The "one" and the "existent" are [mutually] convertible, but as the "existent" is given through an aggregate, and so also is the "one," although the "existent" and the "one" are quasi-mental.[82]

But anything

> which is not one Being on its own account, but an aggregate, and has Arithmetical but not Metaphysical unity.[83]

In this way Leibniz excludes infinite number from the metaphysical world, and feels that he has achieved a reconciliation of infinite monadic plenitude with the paradoxes involved in infinite number.

8. *Continuity*

Leibniz' treatment of what he called the "Labyrinth of the Continuum" can be treated by analogous means—he emerges form this labyrinth by means closely similar to those employed in dealing with the infinite. It is thus advisable to proceed in two stages, first discussing the solution of the mathematical continuum paradox offered by Leibniz, and then how this solution is modified to eliminate the difficulties resulting from various instances of continuity in the metaphysical world.

A. *Mathematical*

Since the machinery used by Leibniz in the solution of this problem is exactly that employed in his treatment of the infinite, there is every reason to suppose that the historical development of the solutions went side by side.[84] Leibniz demanded that a sharp distinction be made between resolution into notions and division into parts, and between what is given as actual and what arises phenomenally. These distinctions he utilizes in his answer to the question of the relation of indivisibles and continuum.

Let us begin with the relation of point to line. Leibniz' position is perfectly explicit, though perhaps somewhat surprising: "A point cannot be a constitutive part of a line."[85] This he explains by application of the remark that an infinite whole actually given does not have ultimately real components; these are mere fictions generated by an indefinite extension of a necessarily finite process.[86] Thus the line "is prior to its point since 'the whole is prior to the part, because the part is only possible and ideal'."[87] And so it transpires that: "Points, to speak precisely, are extremities of extension, and not at all the parts constitutive of things."[88] Leibniz emerges from the mathematical wing of the labyrinth of the continuum by dismissing the problem-task of building a line up out of points.

B. *Metaphysical*

The Leibnizian solution of the metaphysical continuum problem is the complement to the mathematical solution. In the mathematical case difficulty was avoided because what was given as actual or real, the mathematical continuum, could not be composed of points which are mere ideal constructs. In the case of metaphysical reals, i.e., the monads or metaphysical points, difficulty is avoided because these cannot compose a real continuum. Any plurality of monads, has as aggregte a merely phenomenal reality, so that any continuum they can compose is also merely phenomenal. Continuous quantities are thus to be assigned to the realm of phenomenal possibility, not the realm of actualities, except insofar as the actualities involve a determination within possibilities.[89]

As was seen in the mathematical case, continuity occurs "where the parts are indeterminate, and they can be taken in infinitely many [alternative] ways."[90] Thus it follows that:

A continuous quantity is something ideal which pertains to possibles and to actuals—in virtue of their being possibles as well. A continuum, that is, involves indeterminate parts, while, on the other hand, there is nothing indefinite in actual things, in which every division is made that can be made. Actual things are composed as a number is composed of unities, ideal things as a number is composed of fractions; the parts are actual in the real whole but not in the ideal whole. But we confuse ideal with real substances when we seek for actual parts in the order of possibles and indeterminate parts in the aggregate of actuals, and so entangle ourselves in the labyrinth of the continuum and in inexplicable contradictions.[91]

Thus Leibniz holds that a continuum must have indefinite parts, which is something that no collection of monads can have. For:

> An indefinite is something like a continuum whose parts are not [given] in actuality, but can be taken [for consideration] arbitrarily, just like the parts of a unity, or fractions. If there were different subdivisions of organic bodies in nature, there would be different Monads. ...[92]

As Leibniz saw it, the source of the difficulties which constitute the puzzle of the continuum is a failure to distinguish between the ideal or phenomenal and the real or actual. Leibniz grants that there would be trouble if both the indivisible constituent and the continuum to which it belongs could both at once be real, but this, he holds, cannot happen, and thus the collision between indivisible and continuum is prevented. In mathemtics the continuum, the line, is real and the point is merely the ideal limit of an infinite subdivision. In metaphysics only the ultimate constituents, the monads, are actual, and any continuum to which they give rise is but phenomenal.[93] This—in briefest outline—is the Leibnizian solution of the paradoxes of the continuum.

NOTES

1. Leibniz' views on this topic are most completely set forth in correspondence between him and Samuel Clarke during 1715–16, in the course of which Leibniz attacked, anbd Clarke defended, the Newtonian theory of space and time. (For this latter theory see the first scholium of the *Principia*.) For information regarding the occasion of this dispute with Clarke, I refer the reader to Gerhardt's purely historical *Einleitung* to this correspondence (*Phil.*, VII, pp. 347–51; the correspondence itself is given in *Phil.*, VII, pp. 352–440; Loemker, pp. 675–717). We shall draw very heavily on this correspondence for information regarding Leibniz' own views, which are there set forth in considerable detail. He had already contested the Newtonian theory in the *Nouveaux Essais* of 1704 (*Phil.*, V, p. 141).

The roots of the Leibnizian theory of space and time are to be sought in the *Pacidus Philalethi* of 1676 (Couturat, *Opuscules*, pp. 594 ff.). Nevertheless the theory was not, as far as I have been able to discover, formulated prior to 1695. In his objections to the *Système Nouveau* (1695). Foucher writes: "I do not agree with you, that there is any reason to postulate unities which cause the composition and the reality of extension" (*Phil.*, IV, p. 486); for Leibniz had spoken of "unités substantielles" as opposed to mere aggregates seems that the author of the objections did not understand correctly my opinion. Extension or space are only relations [resulting] from order, or orders of coexistence" (*Phil.*, IV, p. 491). This is the first formulation of the Leibnizian theory of space and time I have located, but because this theory rests logically on two ingredients—the theory of monads, and the treatment of the problems of infinity and continuity—both of which were ready circa 1686, I should conjecture that it was developed prior to 1695.

2. Leibniz is so concerned to show that the accord among contemporaneous substances cannot arise by causal influence because, being a mechanist, he could not admit instantaneous causal influence at a distance. He clearly recognized the causal

independence of contemporaries. "If of two elements *which are not simultaneous* one comprehends the cause of the other, the former is considered as preceding, the latter as succeeding," is his definition of temporal order (*Math.*, VII, p. 18; tr. by H. Weil, *Philosophy of Mathematics and Natural Science* [Princeton: Princeton University Press, 1949], p. 101). The theory of relativity has lent interest to this definition. Thus it is via this theory that the definition of events as contemporaries if neither is causally connected with the other is incorporated into Whitehead's "philosophy of organism" (cf. *Process and Reality* [Cambridge: Cambridge University Press, 1929], p. 95). Thus, strangely enough, it is in order to uphold a physical theory of causation—mechanism—that Leibniz is driven to that total denial of causation at the metaphysical level which is formulated in the pre-established harmony.

3. For the principles governing the clarity of perception see *Phil.*, II, p. 90, and *Monadology*, §60.

4. PNG, §2; cf. §11.

5. *Phil.*, II, pp. 450–51.

6. Russell, *Critical Exposition*, p. 122.

7. We have not spoken of "force" as associated with individual substances, nor made much of "Leibniz' dynamism." This is because "force" in the philosophy of Leibniz is a derived notion, resulting from perceptions and their changes. As to dynamism, or the doctrine of unextended centers of force. this ill describes Leibniz' theory of substance since so much more is involved in his individual substances.

8. DM, correspondence with Arnauld

9. "A complete or perfect singular substance involves all its predicates, past, present, and future" (Couturat, *Opuscules*, p. 520).

10 "All singular created substances are diverse expressions of the same universe, ... but the expressions vary in perfection" (Couturat, *Opuscules*, p. 521).

11. 5th letter to Clarke, §47.

12. This is exactly what is now sometimes done in logic in defining a relation as a class of ordered pairs. If this is done, the subject of the relational statement is the, ordered pair and the predicate the assertion of class membership.

13. 5th letter to Clarke, §47.

14. *Math.*, VII, p. 18.

15. Russell, *Critical Exposition*, pp. 64–5. Cf. Buchenau-Cassirer, II, p. 558.

16. Cf. *Monadology*, §§66–9. The nonexistence of a metaphysical vacuum is something necessary, but that of a phenomenal vacuum hinges on the Principle of Perfection.

17. See, for example, the discussion of motion in the *Dynamica, Math.*, VI, pp. 320–6.

18. 3rd letter to Clarke, §5.

19. "Supposing any one should ask, why God did not create everything a year sooner; ... if time was any thing distinct from things existing in time. For it would be impossible there should be any reason, why things should be applied to such particular instants, rather than to others, their succession continuing the same." (*Ibid.*) Cf. the argument of Parmenides (frag. no. 8, Diels) against the createdness of the existent that "if it came from nothing, what need could have made it arise rather later than sooner?"

20. 5th letter to Clarke, §56.

21. "To conceive of extention as something absolute arises from this source, that we conceive of space as a sort of substance, whereas it is no more a substance than is time" (*Phil.*, II, p. 510.)

22. 4th letter to Clarke, §7.

23. "God cannot destroy it, nor even change it in any respect" (*Phil.*, VII, p. 373; 4th letter to Clarke, §10). To hold that space is the *sensorium* of God involves Clarke in theological difficulties, for what need can an omniscient being, who has a *priori* knowledge of all, have of an organ of sensation? Leibniz meets Clarke's efforts at explanation with frigid sarcasm: "I find, in express words, in the Appendix to Sir

Isaac Newton's *Opticks*, that space is the *sensorium* of God. But the word *sensorium* hath always signified the organ of sensation. He, and his friends, may now, if they think fit, explain themselves quite otherwise: I shall not be against it" (2nd letter to Clarke, §3).

24. 4th letter to Clarke, §8.

25. 4th letter to Clarke, §10.

26. 5th letter to Clarke, §38.

27. 5th letter to Clarke, §40. Note that Leibniz' arguments are theological based on the traditional conception of God. Leibniz here deploys his forces with considerable skill. Remark the element of raillery in the following passage: "God's immensity makes him actually present in all spaces. But now if God is in space, how can it be said that space is in God, or that it is a property of God? We have often heard that a property is in its subject; but we never heard, that a subject is in its property" (5th letter to Clarke, §45).

28. This argument appears from the following two passages: "The space taken up by a body, will be the extension of that body. Which is an absurdity; since a body can change space but cannot leave its extension" (5th letter to Clarke, §37). "Everything has its own extension, its own duration; but it has not its own time, and does not keep its own space" (5th letter to Clarke, §46). Further, Leibniz argues that to regard the spatial position of a thing as its property is to commit a rhetorical blunder: "But this is a strange property or affection, which passes from one subject to another" (5th letter to Clarke, §39).

29. See §§47 ff.

30. 5th letter to Clarke, § 47.

31. *Phil.*, II, p. 339.

32. Though Leibniz used both terms there is no conflict. As they arise in the real world space and time are phenomena. As objects of mathematics, "en soy" or apart from the order of real things, they are ideal (5th letter to Clarke, §33).

33. "Nothing of time does ever exist, but instants; and an instant is not even itself a part of time. Whoever considers these observations, will easily apprehend that time can only be an ideal thing" (*Phil.*, VII, p. 402; 5th letter to Clarke, §49).

34. *Math.*, VII, p. 18.

35. "God not only perceives the individual monads and their modifications, but also their relations—and in just this resides their reality. Primary among these (relations) is duration, i.e., the order of successives, and position, i.e., the order of coexistence" (*Phil.*, II, p. 438). The space and time of our perception is a confused, aggregational, version of the space and time seen by God. However, even the latter is phenomenal. It is, furthermore, important to remark that space and time are not, strictly speaking, orders of existents or substances, but orders of created *existents*. God is outside both space and time: "Space is not the place of all things; for it is not the place of God. Otherwise there would be a thing coeternal with God, and independent upon Him; nay, he Himself would depend upon it, if He has need of place" (*Phil.*, p. 409; 5th letter to Clarke, §79).

36. Clearly this argument is circular.

37. *Phil.*, VI, p. 323; *Théodicee*, §351; cf. *Phil.*, III, p. 419.

38. See Clarke's 4th letter, and Leibniz' 5th.

39. Clarke's 4th reply, §§16–17.

40. 5th letter to Clarke, §54.

41. In his 4th letter, Clarke objects "that Time is not merely the Order of things succeeding each other ... because the Quantity of Time may be greater or less, and yet that Order continue the same" (§41). To this Leibniz' reply is: "For if the time is greater, there will be more successive and like states interposed; and if it be less, there will be fewer, seeing there is no vacuum, nor condensation, or penetration (if I may so speak), in times, any more than in places" (5th letter to Clarke, §105).

42. See Couturat, *Opuscules*, p. 610.

43. *Math.*, VII, p. 18.

44. *Nouv. Ess.*, Bk. I, Chap. 15, §11.

45. I quote the most important parts of the passage cited in n. 44: "If there were a void in time, i.e., a duration without any change, it would be impossible to determine its length. ... But one would [then] not be able to refute someone who might say that two successive worlds touch as to duration, so that one begins necessarily when the other ends, without any [intermediate] interval being possible. One would not be able to refute him, I say, because this interval is undeterminable."

46. The reader is referred to the opuscule *De analysis situs* (*Math.*, V, pp. 179–83), and to Chap. 9, "Le Calcul Géométrique," of Couturat, *Logique*. In modern topology, the Leibnizian space is termed an "Umgebungsraum," a "neighborhood-space."

47. "I admit, however, that there is this difference between instants and points—one point of the universe has no advantage of priority over another, while a preceding instant always has the advantage of priority, not merely in time but in nature, over following instants" (*Phil.*, III, pp. 581–82; Loemker, p. 664).

48. That space and time can pertain to the merely possible as well as the actual is clear from *Nouv. Ess.*, Bk. II, ch. xiv, sect. 26.

49. For his dismissal of this prospect see Loemker, p. 263.

50. Jagodinsky, p. 114.

51. "But if there were no creatures, space and time would be only in the ideas of God" (4th letter to Clarke, §41). The case is akin to that of a chessboard when the players play mentally or blindfolded. (See *Phil., V, p. 136.*)

52. Jagodinsky, *loc cit.* The opuscule was written in Paris on 15 April 1676.

53. "[T]here is no spatial or absolute nearness or distance between monads. And to say they are gathered together in a point or disseminated in space is to use certain fictions of our mind." (*Phil.*, II, p. 451; Loemker, p. 604.)

54. "The conservation [of substances] is a perpetual creation ... and all change is a sort of transcreation" (Couturat, *Opuscules*, p. 635).

55. Couturat, *Opuscules*, p. 624; cf. p. 617.

56. *Ibid.*, p. 626.

57. *Phil.*, II, p. 193 (Loemker, p. 521).

58. "That [body] is at rest whose every point remains in the same place. That [body] is in motion which does not rest" (*Math.*, VI, p. 320). One must note that the definition of *place* implies that this defines *relative* motion.

59. *Phil.*, II, p. 270 (Loemker, p. 537). Cf. "... space, time, and motion each are in some degree an *ens rationis*" (*Math.*, VI, p. 247).

60. Couturat, *Opuscules*, p. 590. Leibniz commends Descartes for having insisted on the relative nature of physical motion, but he reproaches him with having neglected this fact in his physics (*Phil.*, IV, p. 369; *Math.*, VI, p. 247).

61. *Phil.*, IV, p. 369; Loemker, p. 393.

62. Clarke's 4th reply, §13.

63. *Ibid.*, p. 403; Loemker, p. 705.

64. This is possible for God alone, our observations giving no clues as to real motion. Hence, for us, an "aequivalentia Hypothesium" prevails here (*Math.*, VI, p. 247).

65. 5th letter to Clarke, §53. To Arnauld, Leibniz writes, "movement of itself, *abstracting from its cause*, is always something relative" (*Phil.*, II, p. 57; Loemker, p. 337). Cf. the following propose definition of motion: "that [body] moves [actually] in which there is present a movement of place [i.e., a relative motion] and moreover a cause (*ratio*) of motion" (*Math.*, VII, p. 20).

66. Again it must be remarked that Leibniz' use of the language of causal efficacy is metaphoric.

67. Couturat, *Opuscules*, p. 606. The reasoning is that the cause of motion must antedate movement.

68. See the remark later written by Leibniz on the ms. of the *Pacidus Philalethi* given in Couturat, *Opuscules*, p. 594.

69. Latta, *op. cit.*, p. 353.

70. 5th letter to Clarke, §53.

71. See, e.g., *Phil.*, VI, p. 29.

72. Math., VII, p. 326. Cp. the Platonic *mēdeis ageōmetētos eisitō*.

73. Thus in the *Meditationes de Cognitione, Veritate et Ideis* of 1684 Leibniz writes: "For we cannot safely (*tuto*) use definitions in deductions before we know that they are real definitions, i.e., that they involve no contradiction. The reason for this is that from notions which involve a contradiction one can simultaneously get opposite results, which are absurd. To make this point I like to us as an example the fastest motion, which implies an absurdity; we posit a wheel among moving with the fastest motion—who doesn't follow me?—[and we also posit] an extended radius of the wheel which, at the end, moves faster than a nail in the circumference of the wheel, whose motion is therefore, contrary to the hypothesis, not the fastest" (*Phil.*, IV, p. 424; Loemker, p. 293).

In the light of later developments the corresponding argument against infinite number is pregnant: "For the greatest number is the same as the number (reading 'numero' for 'numerum'?) of all unities. However, the number of all unities is the same as the number (reading 'numero' for 'numerus') of all numbers. ... Corresponding to any number you please there is given a companion number which is its double. Therefore the number of all numbers is not larger than the number of even numbers; i.e., the whole is not greater than the part" (*Phil.*, I, p. 338).

The property that "the whole is not greater than the part" to which Leibniz objects in infinite collections came to be their defining characteristic. And if one uses the inequality $2^k > k$ instead of $2k \geq k$ in Leibniz' argument against the number of all numbers, it becomes a well-known result of the modern theory of transfinite numbers.

74. *Phil.*, I, p. 338.

75. *Math.*, III, p. 536. Tr. by H. Weil, p. 44. Though Leibniz is not always so precise in his statements, he is quite consistent in his denial of infinitely small quantities. "If dx, d^2x, ... , are, by a certain fiction imagined to remain, even when they become evanescent, as if there were infinitely small *quantities* ..." (J.M. Child, p. 158). Leibniz' position is given in the assertion: "I consider infinitesimal quantities (to be) useful fictions" (*Phil.*, VI, p. 629).

76. In an essay of 1716, probably his last philosophical paper to have survived (see *Phil.*, VI, p. 487), Leibniz writes: "In spite of my Infinitesimal Calculus, I do not at all admit any true infinite number, though I concede that the multitude of things surpasses every finite number, or rather every number" (*Phil.*, VI, p. 629).

77. "I am so much in favor of the actual infinite, that rather than admit that nature abhors it, as one says vulgarly, I hold that nature exemplifies it everywhere, in order to display better the perfections of her author" (*Phil.*, I, p. 416).

78. *Math.*, IV, pp. 94–95.

79. *Phil.*, III, p. 583.

80. *Ibid.*

81. Russell, *Criticial Exposition*, p. 116.

82. *Phil.*, II, p. 304. See the entire letter (to Des Bosses, 1706) (*Phil.*, II, pp. 304 ff.).

83. *Loc. cit.*

84. We chose to consider the problem of infinity first solely because of its logical priority. Note that the dichotomy of the ways of numbering—from ultimate constituents to whole, and from whole to ultimate constituents—parallels the dichotomy of the treatment of continuity into mathematical and metaphysical.

85. G. Wanke, *Das Steitigkeitsgesetz bei Leibniz* (Kiel: Die Universität, 1892), p. 9.

86. "And it is also in this way that mathematical points come into being, (for) they are also only modalities, that is to say extremities. And since everything is indefinite with respect to the abstract line, one here thinks in terms of all that is

possible, such as the fractions of a number, without bothering about any actual divisions of the line" (*Phil.*, IV, p. 491). "And it is the confounding of the ideal with the actual that has completely confused everything, and which has generated the labyrinth [problem] of the 'composition of the continuum.' Those who compose (build up) the line with points have looked for first elements in ideal things, or for connections of a completely inappropriate kind" (*Ibid.*).

87. *Phil.*, IV, p. 492.

88. Wanke, *loc. cit.;* cf. *Phil.*, III. p. 622.

89. See the letter to De Volder of January 19, 1706; *Phil.*, II, pp. 281–283.

90. *Phil.*, IV, p. 392.

91. *Phil.*, II, p. 282; Loemker, p. 539.

92. *Phil.*, II, p. 379.

93. "With regard to those actualities where only genuinely made divisions enter in, the whole is only a result or assemblage (of parts), like a flock of sheep; it is true that the number of simple substances which make up a conglomeration, however small, is infinite, since otherwise the soul which produces the real unity of the animal, the body of a sheep (for example), is genuinely subdivided, that is to say it is also a conglomeration of microscopic animals or plants, themselves composed (of parts) in addition to that which makes their real unity; and since this proceeds to infinity, it is clear that in the end, everything returns to these unities, the remainder or the results being nothing other than well-founded phenomena. ... In actual, substantial things, the whole is a result or assemblage of simple substances, or in other words of a multitude of real unities. And it is the confusion of the ideal with the actual which has confounded everything and produced the labyrinth concerning the composition of the continuum" (*Phil.*, IV, pp. 491–92; Loemker, pp. 535–6). Cf., *Phil.*, II, p. 268, and *Phil.*, III, p. 622.

Chapter XI

Monadic Hierarchies

1. *Structured Aggregates of Monads: Monadic Hierarchy*

A unified aggregate, as we have seen, is a collection of monads whose reciprocal perceptions produce a pervasive condition of clear mutual perception and representation. Speaking in causal terminology, we would say there is a close mutual interaction among the monads of such a group. It is possible, however, for an aggregate to attain to an even higher degree of unity when it is appropriately *structured*. What sort of structuring is at issue here?

Suppose that one monad of a collection perceives the others with a high degree of clarity, a circumstance that perdures through time, so that the changes of state of the other monads are constantly represented with great clarity by the monad at issue. This monad is said by Leibniz to *dominate* the others and to be the *dominant monad* of the collection. Let it be assumed that such as situation is repeated over and over again, somewhat as in the following diagram:

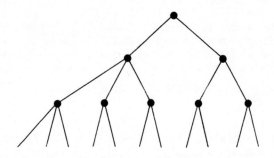

The topmost monad in the dominance hierarchy has access with reasonably high clarity to all or most of the perceptions of the subordinate monads. Here we have the groundwork for the result that

> ... the connection and order of things brings it about that the body of every animal and of every plant is comprised of other animals and of other plants, or of other living and organic beings; consequently there is subordination [of unit to unit], and one body, one substance, serves the other.[1]

Since a single substance provides the focal unifying principle—what Leibniz (adapting an idea of Aristotle's) calls an *entelechy*[2]—we are entitled to consider such a hierarchically structured aggregate as a single individual, as opposed to a merely unified aggregate, such as the one whose "clear perception diagram" might be as follows:

The dominant monad is, so to speak, the central controller for which the others stand in the role of subordinate organs of varying levels of complexity. Because the respective states and changes of state of the whole system, the entire aggregate of monads, and pre-eminently presented in its dominant monad, this pivotal substance creates a unifying *substantial link* for the whole collection. Monadic dominance is, like everything else in Leibniz' world-system, a matter of monadic perception and agreement:

> ... a dominant monad would detract [nothing] from the existence of other monads, since there is really no interaction (*commercium*) between them but merely an agreement (*consensus*). The unity of corporeal substance in a horse does not arise from any "refraction" of the monads but from a superadded substantial bond viz., the dominant monad through which nothing else is changed in the monads themselves.[3]

The interlinkage established dominant monad "uses" the others only figuratively—through their harmony—and not through interaction. Hence the high grade perceptual interconnection established within the dominant monad "is not literally (*essentialiter*) a linkage; it requires the monads but does not essentially involve them, for it could exist without the monads, and the monads without it."[4]

2. *Souls and Spirits*

When a group of monads is so organized that structured aggregate is iteratively piled upon structured aggregate, the highly ramified hierarchic structure that results gives rise to biological organisms. The sequence of cell:organ:plant (or animal) reflects this sort of structurization. When, as in animals (unlike plants), there is a highly centralized structure with one central monad dominating all the rest in its perceptions—ever dominating the dominators of its organic constituents—we see exemplified the mode of monadic organization that typifies man and the higher animals.

In rough correspondence with the common-sense distinction operative in the hierarchy

> men
> animals
> plants
> inert objects

Leibniz distinguishes among various sorts of unified aggregates through their increasing degree of hierarchical organization. In inert objects and at the lower end of the biological scale we find *bare monads*, but in plants and animals we have overriding dominance by a single all-predominant monad. In animals the dominant monad may be called a *soul* (*âme*) and is capable, by way of psychological capabilities, of sensation, consciousness, and memory. In man, and in the higher intelligences of whose existence in nature Leibniz feels assured, the dominant monad is a *spirit* (*esprit*), and is capable of reason, including the practical reason essential to moral agency. For Leibniz, the psychological capabilities and reason itself are functions that come into play at the higher levels of complexity in monadic organization.[5]

The spirits (and souls) that are dominant monads are, like all monads, strictly independent, self-sufficient substances. Why, then, should they have need of a *body*? Of course they do not, strictly speaking, need it at all. But their inclusion in this best of possible worlds gives them a foothold in an orderly cosmos where everything is harmoniously accommodated to everything else within one all-embracing framework of ordering: "If spirits alone existed, they also would lack the requisite interrelation, and would be without the ordering of times and places."[6]

It should not be thought that an animal's dominant monad, for example, is the *permanent* proprietor of the aggregate of monads constituting his body.

> It is true, of course, that a soul cannot pass over from one organic body into another. ... But it must be remembered that even this organic body remains *the same* in the way in which the ship of Theseus or a river does; that is, it is in perpetual flux. And perhaps no portion of matter can be designated which always remains the property of the same animal soul.[7]

Leibniz goes on in this connection to stress:

This does not mean, as some who have misunderstood my thoughts have imagined, that each soul has a quantity or portion of matter appro-priated to it or attached to it forever, and that it consequently owns other inferior beings destined to serve it always; because all bodies are in a state of perpetual flux, like rivers, and the parts are continually entering in or passing out.[8]

With respect to the organization of organic nature, Leibniz drew upon each of the two rival genetic theories of his day: Malpighi's theory of organic preformation and Harvey's theory of epigenesis. According to the theory of preformation, the embryo of an organism is fully formed on a microscopic scale before incubation, the subsequent incubation and development of the organism being simply a matter of growth. In this theory, the entire biological development of an organism is not a matter of any genuine *origination*, but the continued unfolding of a pervasive organic pattern. Opposing this view, the theory of epigenesis—principally derived from microscopic study of the blood—views organisms as genuinely originative from an organic material (the cells) endowed with the capacity for growth, but lacking any predetermined impress of organic form. Leibniz seems to incline towards the theory of preformation at the level of the individual monad with its impressed organic dynamism, and to adopt the standpoint of epigenesis regarding the corporeal bodies of molar organisms.

Since they are monads, souls and spirits of course pre- and post-exist the bodies (monadic aggregates) they come to dominate:

Those souls which one day will be human souls, like those of other species, have been in the seed, and in the progenitors as far back as Adam, and have thus existed always since the beginning of things, in some kind of organic body.[9]

They will ever continue in this best of possible worlds to play some role in the framework of organic nature.

Spirits are unlike the lower monads in that they mirror with relative clarity not only the monads of the created universe, but God as well. The spirits thus constitute the "City of God" which comprises, as we shall see, the locus of moral responsibility and moral goodness in nature.[10]

3. *Minute Perceptions*

The dominant monad of a highly structured hierarchic aggre-gate, which Leibniz characterizes as the *entelechy* of the body represented by the aggregate, has all the monads of all its sub-aggregates (organs) at its disposal with a more than ordinary degree of clarity.[11] Even when the dominance in question is a matter of a spirit's dominance over its body, these perceptions are neither *very* clear nor even conscious. Taken individually, as particular monad-of-monad perceptions, they are never conscious, and thus are never *actual perceptions* in our usual sense of the term. They are *minute perceptions* (*petites perceptions*) which—like the individual impacts of waves lost as individual phenomena when we hear the pounding of the surf—are part of that aggregate phenomenon in which they collectively result. Every perception in our ordinary sense of the term is composed of infinite insensible perceptions.[12] Man's conscious perception is always *confused* perception. It is the aggregate effect of blending innumerable individual perceptions, each of which lies "beneath the threshold" (Leibniz has the concept but does not have this modern term) of noticeability.[13]

The theory of minute (unconscious) perceptions is, with Leibniz, an important part of psychological theory. Even spirits do not always enjoy full-bloodedly conscious perceptions, i.e., apperceptions. In sleep, for example, the dominant monad of a man's mind may or may not be conscious of certain perceptions, contrasting dreams with dreamless sleep. Although Leibniz maintains (with Descartes and against Locke) that a man's mind is always active, he holds (against Descartes) that the "thinking" in question is often altogether unconscious.[14] In the Cartesian view, the continuity of man's psychological life consists of the continuity of thinking, and thus of the unceasing performance of conscious acts. Leibniz, approving Locke's mockery of an insistence upon the continuity of *consciousness*, nevertheless finds psychic continuity in a shading of gradations of perceptions, apperceptions, sensation, and reflexive awareness that range over a wide area in clarity, vividness, and expressiveness, and lie, for the most part, below the horizon of conscious awareness. In holding this theory, Leibniz made a significant innovation in psychological theory to which we will return at greater length.

4. *The Vinculum Substantiale*

Aggregates can become genuinely individuated things, "real unities," only by virtue of the presence of a dominant monad (or *entelechy*), a monad of the system which, because of its hierarchic structuring, can perceive with a high degree of clarity all the other monads of the system. Such a dominant monad provides a sort of central receptor for their perceptions and, so to speak, using them as organs of perception and activity. Only here—in the presence of the "substantial bond" afforded by a dominant monad—do we have an aggregate that is unified sufficiently to deserve the name of an individual thing (substance):

> Monads do not constitute a complete composite substance since they do not make up a unity *per se* but merely an aggregate, unless some substantial bond (*vinculum substantiale*) is added.[15]

Only the highest of the three grades of monads, spirits or minds, are capable of establishing a link which is sufficiently strong to give unity and individuality to the aggregate of monads containing it.[16]

The dominance situated provides the unifying linkage, the substantial bond (*vinculum substantiale*) which enables the aggregate of monads to attain to substantial form or substantial unity.[17] A body without a dominant *entelechy* is merely a thing of aggregation, but with appropriate dominance it ceases to be a mere aggregate and becomes a true unity. The dominant monad creates a substantial bond among the intrinsically separate monads of the system, fusing them into a genuinely organic unit, and leading to a pluri-monadic entity that has authentic and intrinsic unity, and not merely an apparent unity for an external perceiver.

Two cases can accordingly be distinguished:

> [E]ither bodies are mere phenomena, in which case extension too will be only a phenomenon and only monads will be real, but the union will be supplied in the phenomenon by the action of the perceiving soul; or ... substance consists in that unifying reality which adds something absolute and hence substantial, even though fluid, to the things to be united.[18]

Leibniz's correspondence with Father des Bosses, who taught the theology at the Jesuit school at Hildesheim, is of fundamental importance for an understanding of this aspect of his metaphysics.[19] It is here that, in the course of a discussion of the dogma of trans-substantiation, Leibniz develops in detail his concept of a *vinculum substantiale*, a bond that can fuse into organized composite wholes the "windowless" monads which are the ontological basis of his metaphysical system. Leibniz' motives in espousing the views he presents in this correspondence with des Bosses were called into question by Russell:

> In later letters, the doctrine [of the *vinculum substantiale*] is usually

presupposed as the basis of discussion, and is employed to establish real matter and a real continuum. But nowhere does Leibniz himself assert that he believes it. He was extremely anxious to persuade Catholics that they might, without heresy, believe in his doctrine of monads. Thus the *vinculum substantiale* is rather the concession of a diplomatist than the creed of a philosopher.[20]

In view of this rebuke, classing the doctrine of a *vinculum substantiale* as a gratuitous feature of his philosophy introduced to accommodate the Catholics, it is of interest to note that the contentions of Leibniz to which Russell objects are all to be found in Leibniz' correspondence regarding some points in the philosophy of physics with Burcher de Volder, a Cartesian who taught mathematics, physics, and philosophy at Leyden.[21] Though Leibniz does not here use the term *vinculum substantiale*, he presents all essentials of the doctrine in question. Moreover, Russell's doubt is quixotic on the very face of it: a man who explains to another at great length how the land lies need not make an issue of adding that this is how he believes it to lie. After all, the idea of a substantial bond is simply a systematic elaboration of the idea of monadic dominance. And consequently the position at issue in Leibniz' conception of a *vinculum substantiale* was not "the concession of a diplomatist," but the exfoliation by a philosophical system-builder of an essential facet of his position.

NOTES

1. *Théodicée*, §200.
2. The term *entelechy* is sometimes applied 'by Leibniz to monads generally (e.g., *Monadology*, §56), but is usually restricted by him to monads capable of dominance, i.e., to souls and spirits.
3. *Phil.*, II, p. 452.
4. *Phil.*, V, p. 516.
5. The angels (i.e., higher-than-human created rational beings) all have bodies (*Phil.*, II, p. 324). God alone is a pure, wholly incorporeal spirit (*Phil.*, VI, p. 546; cf. *Nouv. Ess.*, Bk. II, Chap. i, §12).
6. *Théodicée*, §120.
7. *Phil.*, II, p. 370 (Loemker, p. 597).
8. *Monadology*, §72.
9. *Phil.*, VI, p. 152; *Théodicée*, §91.
10. PNG, §§84–9. It is problematic for Leibniz whether a spirit ever *fully* loses its body (i.e., ceases to dominate some aggregate of monads). He inclines to answer the question in the negative. See p. 120.
11. The expression "primitive entelechy" is, however, used by Leibniz to apply generically to *any* monad.
12. *Nouv. Ess.*, Bk. I, chap. 1, §§15–17.
13. *Clear* perception in Leibniz is always a matter of monad-of-monad perception

and, in the case of created monads, is (unlike *apperception+ self-perception*) never conscious, save in the aggregate.

14. *Nouv. Ess.*, Bk. II, chap. 19, §4.

15. *Phil.*, II, p. 444; Loemker, p. 602.

16. "... bodies are made only for spirits alone ..." (*Phil.*, IV, p. 485). Leibniz is somewhat inconsistent here in limiting the type of monad capable of dominance to *spirits*; generally it seems that both spirits and souls are able to dominate a system of monads—spirits for men, souls for animals.

17. The justification of this presentation of the matter of to be found in the correspondence with Arnauld (*passim*), in the *Système Nouveau*, and in the correspondence with des Bosses (*passim*). On the relevant issues see A. Boehm's *Le "Vinculum Substantiale" chez Leibniz* (Paris: J. Vrin, 1938).

18. *Phil.*, II, pp. 435–6; Loemker, p. 600.

19. This correspodence is given in *Phil.*, II and in Loemker, pp. 596–617.

20. Russell, *Critical Exposition*, p. 152.

21. Also given in *Phil.*, II and in Loemker, pp. 515–41.

Chapter XII

Human Knowledge

1. *Truths of Fact and Truths of Reason*

The dichotomy of truths of fact (*vérités de fait*) and truths of reason (*vérités de raison*) is the cornerstone of Leibniz' theory of knowledge. Truths of fact deal specifically with the *actual* world. The grounds of these truths of fact hinge upon the will of God—they would be falsehoods rather than truths had He chosen it so, but we humans are wholly reliant upon experience for our acquaintance with them, for we can obtain knowledge of such truths only through perception: "[O]nly God knows the contingent truths *a priori* and sees their infallibility otherwise than by experience."[1] God alone can terminate the infinite analysis through which they can be established—but only with relative necessity—with respect to the Principle of Perfection. On the other hand, truths of reason do not deal with matters of contingent existence but with universal facts that must hold good in *every* possible world.[2] (There is but one existential truth of this noncontingent character, namely that which asserts the existence of God.) Knowledge of such necessary truths is available, even to man, by conceptual analysis of a finitistic character. The status of these truths is independent of the will of God; they are as they are because the concepts involved in them are what they are.

The most crucial facet of Leibniz' theory of knowledge is the epistemological dualism inherent in this theory of truth. As regards human (in contrast to divine) epistemology, there are then two distinct paths leading to two types of truth: perception (and apperception) leading, when employed to two types of properly, to truths of fact, and analytical reason leading, when correctly used, to truths of reason. To be sure, even contingent truths of fact are analytic—but only infinitely so, in a manner accessible to God alone. His knowledge of the world can proceed via complete individual notions; ours cannot. Our only access to the truths of fact is through *experience*. In all matters of factual knowledge about the contingent arrangements of this world, Leibniz is fully committed to empiricism. If holding that only by observational experience can man obtain knowledge of "matters of fact and existence" makes the empiricist, then Leibniz is as much an empiricist as any.

2. *Perception and Apperception*

Since we have dealt with perception thus far only in the generic way applicable unrestrictedly to all monads, special consideration must be given to some of its further ramifications. Four must be distinguished: (1) *ordinary monadic perception* as based on the mutual representation of all monads; (2) *minute* (i.e., unconscious) *perception* by the higher-grade monads of other monads; (3) the *confused perception* by the higher grade monads of monadic aggregates; (4) *apperception*, the reflexive self-perception of spirits. Monadic perception in its elemental sense, based on the fact that the monads, though windowless, accord with one another in this best of possible worlds, applies throughout the monadic realm. The other modes, however, apply only to monads of the higher grades (viz., souls and spirits) and come into play only when these monads are the dominant monads of suitably complex aggregated organisms.

Minute perception and confused perception go hand in hand. When the dominant monad of a high-grade aggregate perceives confusedly the monads constituting some other aggregates, it perceives minutely some or most of the individual monads that constitute this aggregate. (Prosaically, when I, i.e., my dominant monad, see a chair, i.e., the monadic aggregate constituting the chair, then I in fact perceive confusedly the monads constituting the surface of the chair on my perspectival side—minutely perceiving them as individuals, but blurring these minute discrete perceptions into a confused whole.)

Leibniz succinctly characterizes apperception in the following terms:

> Thus it is well to distinguish between *perception*, which is the interior state of the monad representing outer things, and *apperception*, which is [self-] consciousness or the reflexive [or *reflective*] knowledge of this inner state.[3]

Apperception requires consciousness; it is the mode of perception distinctive of monads of the highest grade, the spirits. Apperception, however, is not consciousness as such (which is present in souls as well as spirits, in animals as well as man), but self-conciousness or self-perception generally, involving the capacity for reflexive self-revealing perception of the workings of one's own mind.[4] The procedure of some commentators in equating apperception with *conscious perception* in general[5] is not faithful to Leibniz' own equation: apperception = *inner-directed perception.* Leibniz' distinction between perception and apperception is in strict parallel to Locke's distinction between sensation and reflection, with consciousness in general present on both sides of the boundary, operative in regard to our awareness of both external things and internal states.

3. *Memory*

Memory, for Leibniz, comes near to being a cross between perception and apperception. In perception a (i.e., any) monad represents the states of other monads; in apperception a (highest-grade) monad reflects the contemporary state of itself; with memory the higher-grade monads (souls and spirits) simply reflect states of their own past, generally in a confused way.

Memory is the key to the individuation through time of the spirits (minds; *esprits*), i.e., their continuing self-identity *as spirits.* As a monad, every spirit has a definitive, complete historically continuous self-identity built into its characterizing program, but this would not guarantee its permanence and continuing self-identity as a spirit, rather than merely as a substance. When in the course of its history a monad once attains to the status of a spirit, coming to dominate a suitably complex aggregate of monads, it retains this status forever (for reasons to be explored later, but ultimately vouched for only by the fact that this is the best of possible worlds). It will always retain some suitable retinue of monads to dominate, perhaps dropping for a time to the status of a lower-grade soul, but never losing its status as a better than bare (inorganic) monad, and never losing its capacity for dominance of high-level complex aggregates. Moreover, a spirit never wholly loses the memory of its conscious experiences, although this memory may itself lapse into unconsciousness for stretches of time. A spirit can always look forward to future periods of high-level activity.

Leibniz' teaching of the permanently elect status of spirits is partly a matter of theological accommodation. It is not a theorem, but a side-product of the system; it is no more than a somewhat tendentious construction of the sort of goodness at issue in the best possible world.

4. *Innate Truths and Ideas*

Man's experiential knowledge of particular facts about the realm of contingent existence is never *distinct* in the technical sense of this term which Leibniz adapted from Descartes:

> Knowledge is clear, therefore, rather than obscure when it makes it possible for me to recognize the thing represented. Clear knowledge, in turn, is either confused or distinct. It is *confused* when I cannot enumerate one by one the marks which are sufficient to distinguish the thing from others, even though the thing may in truth have such marks and constituents into which its concept can be resolved. Thus we know colors, odors, flavors, ... A distinct concept, however, is the kind of notion which assayers have of gold; one namely which enables them to distinguish gold from all other bodies by sufficient marks and observations.[6]

It is thus evident that man can never attain to better than confused (albeit clear) knowledge regarding contingent particulars, their nature (i.e., individual notions) being accessible to us only incompletely in piecemeal experience.

The case differs as regard the truths of reason, where we deal not with categorical truths about existing substances, but with (1) *hypothetical* truths about possible (or actual, the distinction is now indifferent) substances ("If Caesar is a general, and Caesar is in Rome, then a general is in Rome"), and (2) categorical truths about, not *substances*, but abstract *concepts* ("Primes greater than two are odd integers"). The first category reduces to the second, what is at issue always being a generic principle in which no essential reference to the specific substances being mentioned is involved ("If anything is an X, and moreover is in place P, then an X is in place P").[7]

Even when their subject matter is perceptual, such abstract truths do not really hinge on perception: they do not depend upon any features of the actual world. Thus truths of the type "The sweet is not bitter" and "The red is not green" are analytic truths, truths of reason. This is due, from an epistemological angle, to their strictly hypothetical nature. Once one recognizes, however obscurely, the concepts involved (sweet, red), which represent matters met with only in the realm of sense experience, *then* one needs no *further* experience to validate the truth at issue, but can do so solely by analysis of the now *ex hypothesi* known concepts.

In contrast with the truths of reason dealing with such sensory *concepts*—though not, of course, sensory *facts*—there is a second, more important category of truths of reason which Leibniz calls innate truths (*vérités innées*).[8] These innate truths deal with innate ideas, that is, with idealizations recognized by the mind through reflexive probing into its own contents.[9] Such truths—those of mathematics, for example—do not deal specifically with the things of this world, but with those pertaining equally to every possible world.

The necessary truths of reason are "independent of perception" not in the sense that we may not learn of them in the course of experience, but that such experiences play a heuristic and not a determinative role. Leibniz' analogy is that experience helps us to such innate truths in the way in which miners come to expose a vein of ore, not by creating it as a result of their work as, for example, a painter does, but by exposing a pre-existing material whose nature is wholly independent of their efforts and merely revealed by them. In holding that the concepts at issue in certain truths of reason are innate ideas, Leibniz does not mean to assert that infants are aware of them (that babies know about squares, circles and numbers, for example). To be called innate, an idea or truth need not actually be known: it need simply be accessible in virtue of the mind's own conceptual resources.

Why did Leibniz not hold *all* ideas and *all* truths to be innate, as Russell contends he ought to have done?

> To the general theory that all truths which are known are innate, which Leibniz should have adopted, there is no answer but one which attacks the whole doctrine of monads.[10]

This criticism overlooks the important fact that Leibniz' conception of the innate is best construed in a contentual rather than a temporal sense. Granted, all that happens to any monad, all its perception and knowledge of truths of fact and truths of reason alike is eternally encapsulated within its defining complete individual notion. However, some of its perceptions are outward-oriented to other substances (what philosophers nowadays call *intentional*) and some are inward-oriented to itself (apperception). Certain ideas and truths are thus rendered innate, not by their failure to be built into a monad a priori, but by being wholly independent (logically rather than chronologically) of perceptions of the outward-oriented, intentional type.

Leibniz is thus able to draw the distinction between "innate" and "acquired" ideas and truths wholly *within* the ambit of his theory of complete, all-embracing individual notions. His reconstruction of such a term as "innate" may be somewhat artificial, but this artificiality is at any rate perfectly harmless to the self-consistency and conceptual viability of his system.

5. *The Role of Reason*

With respect to the epistemology of human knowledge, Leibniz distinguishes three faculties: sense, imagination, and reason.[11] Sense deals with the sensory qualities encountered in the perception of external objects. The imagination, classed as an *internal sense*, adds to the individual senses the deliverances of the common sense, and thus introduces the "common sensibles" that provide the materials of mathematics. Reason brings us to the super-sensible, i.e., the apperception of the mind's functioning even when not engaged in working with sensory materials.

The materials of the truths of fact derive from sensation (i.e., conscious external perception); those of the pure truths of reason (innate truths) are inherent, and based, or at any rate basable, upon apperception. Knowledge of truths of reason is thus confined to spirits; souls (therefore the higher animals below man) are capable of sensation, consciousness (*attentio*), and memory,[12] but not of apperception, i.e., the *self*-consciousness requisite to apprehension of innate ideas. Here we encounter the materials for logic and metaphysics as well as the fundamental conceptions of ethics.

Leibniz accordingly holds that there are two empirical sources of data for knowledge, external and internal perception (reflection). The former gives the basis for scientific knowledge, but the latter alone supplies the materials for logic, for mathematics, and moreover, for metaphysics, since it is the ultimate source of our knowledge of such categories as substance and causality, and also provides the foundation of the "personal identity" needed for moral responsibility, as distinguished from metaphysical or monadic identity. (To know the latter would require a knowledge of the law of one's individual nature).

Reason has two basic capacities with respect to its materials, the ideas: *analysis*, by which these ideas are dissected into their component ideas, and *comparison*, by which the coincidences and differences between the components of two ideas can be noted. The fundamental resources of human reasoning are extremely simple, but their systematic, component application leads to the endless complexities of our knowledge.

Notwithstanding his classification as a rationalist, Leibniz does not think that any empirical science can be deduced from metaphysical first principles. He does think of the empirical facts as "grounded in" metaphysical truths (via the Principle of Sufficient Reason),[13] but *deduction* is no more at issue here than Kant believed that Newtonian astronomy can be deduced from the Principle of Causality. The principles in each case provide only the general framework for a generic *mode* of justification. Leibniz leaves no room for doubt that on the side of *human* epistemology, he is a strict empiricist; the detailed content of an empirical science must be obtained through experimentation and observation.

6. *Universal Science*

Always important in his thinking about the task of reason was Leibniz' program of a universal science (*scientia universalis*) for coordinating all human knowledge, providing an architectonic framework within which each of the particular sciences, while functioning efficiently in its own area, would stand in illuminating relation to the rest. This program comprised two parts: (1) a universal character or notation (*characteristica universalis*) by use of which any item of information can be recorded in a natural, simple, and systematic way, and (2) a formalized method or calculus for reasoning (*calculus ratiocinator*), manipulating the knowledge recorded in a computational fashion to reveal the logical consequences of any item and its interrelation with others. The project of a universal character was to serve several functions: provide a simplified notation for science, a medium of international communication, and a ready source of information to facilitate scientific discovery and demonstration. It was by no means original with Leibniz, but was, as one recent scholar puts it, "an intellectual commonplace in seventeenth century Western Europe."[14] The conception of a calculus ratiocinator, however, was original with Leibniz, and led him to develop mathematically inspired systems for reasoning in a way that makes him the unquestioned founder of modern symbolic logic.[15]

In his early *Dissertation on the Art of Combinations*[16] Leibniz sought to take steps toward developing "science of the sciences" along mathematico-logical lines. He worked in terms of his subsequently standard approach of beginning with basic general concepts and, by their combination, building up complexes which can then be analyzed into their basic constituents. This combinatorial procedure underwrites the possibility of substituting mathematical computation for conceptual analysis, for "characters can be applied to ratiocination [because] there is in them a kind of complex mutual placing (*situs*) or order which fits the things [represented], if not in the single words at least in their combination and connection."[17]

For the purposes of a somewhat crude illustration, consider the correspondence of concepts to index-numbers:

> 2–dog
> 6–spaniel
> 7–male
> 11–female

A *female spaniel* would get the index-number $66 = 6 \times 11$. The fact that this includes 2 among its divisors, the index-number for *dogs*, underwrites the truth of the proposition that *Every female spaniel is a dog*. With this approach we could also guarantee through computation the validity of such a syllogistic inference as

$$\frac{\text{All } M \text{ is } P}{\begin{array}{c} \text{All } S \text{ is } M \\ \hline \text{All } S \text{ is } P \end{array}}$$

Since when we know that $\#(P)$, the index-number for P, is a divisor of $\#(M)$, and that $\#(M)$ is a divisor of $\#(S)$, $\#(P)$ must also be a divisor of $\#(S)$. Development of complex arithmetical schemes for the accommodation of logical inferences was a lifelong preoccupation which Leibniz carried to a high degree of sophistication and adequacy.

7. *Error*

In regard to truths of reason, error can come about only through heedlessness or carelessness—that is, through an outright mistake. This can occur (1) in the analysis of a concept by an oversight or omission of something that belongs to it or by the careless or inadvertent insertion of something that does not, or (2) in the comparison of two concepts, either in erroneously finding a feature in one concept in which it is not really present, or in failure to note that a feature actually present in one is also present in the other. Errors concerning truths of reason thus come about essentially either through mistakes in calculation (due to lack of attention) or in memory:

> There can be no doubt in mathematical demonstrations except insofar as we need to guard against error in our arithmetical calculations. For this there is no remedy except to re-examine the calculation frequently or to have it tested by others so as to add confirmatory proofs. This weakness of the human mind arises from a lack of attention and memory and

cannot be completely overcome, and Descartes' allusion to it, as if he knew of a remedy, is in vain.[18]

The mention of lack of attention points to carelessness as a prime source of error in this sphere, and mention of memory points to Leibniz' Platonic doctrine that the truths of reason lie buried in the unconscious recesses of man's memory.

Error in regard to truths of fact comes about through illusion or delusion. Either (1) we may mistake what we sense, imputing to some actual external aggregate of monads, on inadequate or misinterpreted sensory evidence, a feature which does not reflect the actual condition of the aggregate (as, for example, in a case of mistaken identity; this possibility is built into the confused nature of perception); (2) we may, in the case of outright delusion, simply impute to the external world of monads aggregational features for which there is no adequate basis (e.g., a mirage), that is, which have no appropriate basis external to the misperceiving monad. This second is never, as with Descartes, a matter of sheer willfulness without any adequate basis whatsoever, but always has *some* foundation, however tenuous, in the sphere of monadic realities.

8. *The Unconscious*

Leibniz' doctrine of unconscious perception (*petite perception*) may be seen as a bold stroke of innovative genius in the history of psychology, but it may also be seen in the less dazzling light of an inescapable necessity of Leibniz' system. Consider two of Leibniz' commitments: (1) every monad always perceives (the contemporaneous state of) every other monad with a greater or lesser degree of clarity; (2) the human mind is a monad—the dominant monad of the highly structured aggregate that is the human body. Given these two commitments, the concept of unconscious perception is, for all practical purposes, an unavoidable result. They demand a theory that admits of perceptions below the threshold of conscious awareness.

As opposed to Locke, Leibniz maintains the Cartesian teaching that the spirit always thinks. This thought, however, need not be conscious. A spirit (like any monad) will never be without perceptions, but will often be without *apperceptions* (conscious perceptions), whenever, for example, we have no distinct perceptions, as in deep sleep.[19] The unconscious as it relates to *petites perceptions* in Leibniz' theory of psychology is not, of course, to be thought of along Freudian lines. Rather, it can be viewed in light of the Fechner-Weber approach in explaining conscious molar experiences by reference to their origin in micro-events serving as their stimuli at the physiological level.

The higher-grade monads (souls and spirits) are capable of memory, i.e., perceiving stages of their own past. Traces of all that happens to such monads at one juncture are found at all later junctures. But the monads are not always consciously aware of their entire past; the retrospective perceptions are for the most part very weak, and entirely unconscious. Nevertheless, the *petites perceptions* play a very important role in providing for the continuity of psychic life:[20]

> These insensible perceptions also identify and constitute the same individual who is characterized by the traces or expressions which they preserve of the preceding states of this individual, in connecting them with his present state. ... But they (namely these perceptions) even provide the means for recovering this recollection. ... It is for this reason that death can only be a sleep and cannot indeed continue, the perceptions merely ceasing to be sufficiently distinguished, and reduced in animals to a state of confusion which suspends consciousness, but which cannot last always; not to speak here of man who must in this regard have great privileges in order to preserve his personality.[21]

Leibniz specifically likens man's physiological state of "losing consciousness" in periods of fainting or dreamless sleep, during which we have no distinct apperception and of which we later remember nothing, with the ordinary perceptions of the bare monads from which this "does not sensibly differ."[22]

Not only can a man's mind (*spirit; esprit*) have unconscious perceptions—a feature it share with the soul (*âme*) of an animal—but it can also have unconscious apperceptions. This is somewhat surprising; it might seem that when we are self-conscious (i.e., aware of being aware of something) we must *ipso facto* be aware of this awareness. But against this view Leibiz redeploys the infinite regress argument, already found in Aristotle,[23] to the effect that:

> it is impossible for us always to reflect explicitly upon [i.e., be reflexively aware of] all of our thoughts; otherwise the mind would make a reflexion upon each reflexion *ad infinitum*, without ever being able to pass on to a new thought.[24]

The iterative piling-up of reflective awareness of reflective awareness must stop somewhere, and the conception of unconscious apperception provides a convenient means of termination.

As these explanations indicate, Leibniz does not give the unconscious a prominent place in his account of the psychology of spirits on grounds of any specifically empirical investigation of actual features of human perception and thought. He was compelled to the development of his theory of the unconscious by the systematic exigencies of his metaphysical view of the mind as a monad.

9. Scientific Method

How are human inquirers, bereft of adequate insight into the nature of things, to come into the possession of truths of fact? Where *particular* truths are concerned, the mechanisms of perception and apperception will serve. But this will clearly not be adequate to the attainment of *general* truths. How can we proceed here?

Leibniz characterizes the proper method here as "the conjectural method *a priori*" which "proceeds by hypotheses, assuming certain causes, perhaps without proof [i.e., *direct* evidence], and showing that the things which actually happen would follow from these assumptions."[25] It is conjectural because of its crucial reliance on *hypotheses*, and *a priori* because of its reliance on fundamental principles whose establishment lies beyond the reach of induction. The apriority at issue here indicates not the *dispensibility* of the empirical, but its insufficiency to the task at hand with *demonstrating* the conclusion:

> For perfectly universal propositions can never be established on this basis [viz., induction based on the experience of particular cases] because you are never certain in induction that all individuals have been considered. You must always stop at the proposition that all the cases which I have experienced are so. But since, then, no true universality is possible, it will always remain possible that countless other cases which you have not examined are different. But, you may ask, do we not say universally that fire—that is, a certain luminous, fluid, subtle body, usually flares up and burns when wood is kindled, even if no one has examined all such fires, because we have found it to be so in those cases we have examined? That is, we infer from them, and believe with moral certainty, that all fires of this kind burn and will burn you if you put your hand to them. But this moral certainty is not based on induction alone and cannot be wrested from it by main force but only by the addition or support of the following universal propositions, which do not depend on induction but on a universal idea or definition of terms: (1) *if the cause is the same or similar in all cases, the effect will be the same or similar in all*; (2) *the existence of a thing which is not sensed is not assumed*; and, finally, (3) *whatever is not assumed, is to be disregarded*

in practice until it is proved. From these principles arises the practical or moral certainty of the proposition that all such fire burns. ... Hence it is clear that induction in itself produces nothing, not even any moral certainty, without the help of propositions depending not on induction but on universal reason. For if these helping propositions, too, were derived from induction, they would need new helping propositions, and so on to infinity, and moral certainty would never be attained.[26]

The fact that the method relies crucially on conjectures whose full content lies beyond the reach of reasonable experience means that no reason in the domain of the probable, the less-than-*metaphysically*-certain. But the method can assuredly attain the *morally* certain—let alone the *practically* certainty which suffices for the guidance of affairs in everyday life.

Some hypotheses can satisfy so many phenomena, and so easily, that they can be taken for certain. Among other hypotheses, those are to be chosen which are the simpler; these are to be presented, in the interim, in place of the true causes
The conjectual method a priori proceeds by hypotheses, assuming certain causes, perhaps without proof, and showing that the things which actually happen would follow from these assumptions. A hypothesis of this kind is like the key to a cryptograph, and the simpler it is, and the greater the number of events that can be explained by it, the more probable it is. But just as it is possible to write a letter intentionally so that it can be understood by means of several different keys, of which only one is the true one, so the same effect can have several causes. Hence no firm demonstration can be made from the success of hypotheses. Yet I shall not deny that the number of phenomena which are happily explained by a given hypothesis may be so great that it must be taken as morally certain. Indeed, hypotheses of these kind are sufficient for everyday use. Yet it is also useful to apply less perfect hypotheses as substitutes for truth until a better one occurs, that is, one which explains the same phenomena more happily or more phenomena with equal felicity. There is no danger in this if we carefully distinguish the certain from the probable.[27]

The degree of probability that is attained through the conjectural method will hinge on the nature of the conjectural hypotheses at which the method arrives:

Yet it must be admitted that a hypothesis becomes the more probable as it is simpler to understand and wider in force and power, that is, the greater the number of phenomena that can be explained by it, and the fewer the further assumptions. It may even turn out that a certain hypothesis can be accepted as physically certain [*pro physice certa*] if, namely, it completely satisfies all the phenomena which occur, as does the key to a cryptograph. Those hypotheses deserve the highest praise (next to truth), however, by those aid predictions can be made, even about phenomena or observations which have not been tested before; for a hypothesis of this kind can be applied, in practice, in place of truth.[28]

Leibniz' exposition of the "conjectural method *a priori*" makes it clear that what is at issue here is exactly what has become known as the hypothetico-deductive method of scientific method. And his account of this method and its *modus operandi* is such that his traditional ranking as a "Rationalist" is highly problematical. In his emphasis on the dependence of factual knowledge upon observation, his concerns for experimental design, and his views on the nature of hypotheses and the principles for their assessment, Leibniz is a rigorous empiricist.

10. *Leibniz as Pioneer of the Coherence Theory of Truth*

In turning from metaphysics to epistemology we leave the God's-eye perspective behind. Our concern is thus not with the God-oriented issue of which existential possibility is to be real (i.e., realized) but with the very human problem of which among the many possibilities that seem so to us are actually real. The problem now is not which ontological possibility is to be actualized but which epistemological possibility in the *phenomenal* sphere is to be recognized as actual—i.e., veridical.

Leibniz treats this epistemological issue in one of his most powerfully seminal works, the little tract *De modo distinguendi phaenomena realia ab imaginariis*. How does the golden mountain I imagine differ from the real earthern, rocky, and wooden mountain I see yonder? Primarily in two respects: internal detail and general conformity to the course of nature. Regarding the internal detail of vividness and complexity Leibniz says:

> We conclude it from the phenomenon itself if it is vivid, complex, and internally coherent [*congruum*]. It will be vivid if its qualities, such as light, color, and warmth, appear intense enough. It will be complex if these qualities are varied and support us in undertaking many experiments and new observations; for example, if we experience in a phenomenon not merely colors but also sounds, odors, and qualities of taste and touch, and this both in the phenomenon as a whole and in its various parts which we can further treat according to causes. Such a long chain of observations is usually begun by design and selectively and usually occurs neither in dreams nor in those imaginings which memory or fantasy present, in which the image is mostly vague and disappears while we are examining it.[29]

Regarding the second aspect of coherence, Leibniz says:

> A phenomenon will be coherent when it consists of many phenomena,

for which a reason can be given either within themselves or by some sufficiently simply hypothesis common to them; next, it is coherent if it conforms to the customary nature of other phenomena which have repeatedly occurred to us, so that its parts have the same position, order, and outcome in relation to the phenomenon which similar phenomena have had. Otherwise phenomena will be suspect, for if we were to see men moving through the air astride the hippogryphs of Ariostus, it would, I believe, make us uncertain whether we were dreaming or awake.[30]

He elaborates this criterion in considerable detail:

But this criterion can be referred back to another general class of tests drawn from preceding phenomena. The present phenomenon must be coherent with these if, namely, it preserves the same consistency or if a reason can be supplied for it from preceding phenomena or if all together are coherent with the same hypothesis, as if with a common cause. But certainly a most valid criterion is a consensus with the whole sequence of life, especially if many others affirm the same thing to be coherent with their phenomena also, for it is not only probable but certain, as I will show directly, that other substances exist which are similar to us. Yet the most powerful criterion of the reality of phenomena, sufficient even by itself, is success in predicting future phenomena from past and present ones, whether that prediction is based upon a reason, upon a hypothesis that was previously successful, or upon the customary consistency of things as observed previously.[31]

Thus Leibniz lays down two fundamental criteria for the distinguishing of real from imaginary phenomena; the vividness and complexity of inner detail on the one hand and the coherence and lawfulness of mutual relationship upon the other.

Now the interesting and striking fact about this sector of Leibnizian epistemology is *its complete parallelism* with his ethical metaphysics of creation. In both cases alike, the operative criterion of the real resides in a combination of variety and orderliness. This is certainly no accident. One cannot but sense the deep connection at work here. Let us attempt to illuminate it.

Leibniz's line of thought begins with a theologico-metaphysical application of ethical theory: the doctrine that God will chose for actualization that one among all possible worlds which qualifies as "the best." The implementation of this doctrine, of course, calls for a *metaphysical standard of relative perfection*, a requirement filled by the Leibnizian criterion of lawfulness and variety.

Given this starting-point it is natural to invoke the logical principle of *adaequatio intellectu ad rem* to the effect that, as Spinoza puts it, "the order and connection of ideas is the same as the order and connection of things." Appeal to this principle serves to transmute our metaphysical standard of perfection as used ontologically for bridging the metaphysical division between *possibility and reality* into an epistemological standard for bridging the division between *appearance and reality*. In this way, Leibniz shifts the application of the fundamental criterion of variety and orderliness from God's realization-selection of a real among possible worlds to man's recognition-selection of a real among apparent phenomena.

Leibniz's line of thought thus in effect exhibits the striking feature of using a logical doctrine, the correspondence theory of truth and reality (*adaequatio intelletu ad rem*), to validate an epistemological coherence theory of truth and reality in terms of the ethico-metaphysical standard of perfection that he views as operative in God's creation choice. This complex and fruitful conjoining of different elements is altogether typical of Leibniz's ingenuity as a philosophic system-builder.

The coherence theory of truth has plays a central role in thinking of the Anglo-American idealists from Bradley, Bosanquet, and Joachim to A.C. Ewing and Brand Blanshard in our own day. Moreover this theory of truth has had a definite appeal for some members of the Vienna school of logical positivism (O. Neurath, R. Carnap [at one brief stage], C.G. Hempel [in some passages]). There is no time here to enter into details.[32] But it is relevant to our present concerns to note that the modern coherence theorists articulate a criterion of truth that revolves around exactly the two Leibnizian factors of variety and order.

By way of illustration, consider the best-known idealist exponent of the coherence theory, the English metaphysician F.H. Bradley, who writes as follows:

> There is a misunderstanding against which the reader must be warned most emphatically. The test which I advocate is the idea of a whole of knowledge as wide and as consistent as may be. In speaking of system I mean always the union of these two aspects, and this is the sense and the only sense in which I am defending coherence. If we separate coherence from what Prof. Stout calls comprehensiveness, then I agree that neither of these aspects of system will work by itself. How they are connected, and whether in the end we have one principle or two, is of course a difficult question. ... All that I can do here is to point out that both of the above aspects are for me inseparably included in the idea of system, and that coherence apart from comprehensiveness is not for me the test of truth or reality.[33]

Bradley thus insists emphatically upon conjoining in his own coherence criterion of truth exactly the two Leibnizian factors of order (=coherence) and variety (=comprehensiveness).

These very brief indications should, I think, suffice to show that Leibniz must be viewed as a pioneer of this line of thought and he beyond question qualifies as one of the fathers of the coherence theory of truth.

There is, to be sure, a crucial difference between Leibniz and the English neo-Hegelians who espoused the coherence theory of truth at the end of the last century. They are separated by the vast gulf of Kant's Copernican Revolution.

Unlike Leibniz, the modern idealists usually abandoned altogether the traditional correspondence-to-fact idea of truth, and looked upon coherence as affording not an epistemological *criterion* of truth but a logical *definition* of it. They gave up as useless baggage the whole idea of correspondence with an *an sich* reality. This, of course, is a position which Leibniz was unable to take, so that, naturally enough, he remained in the pre-Kantian dogmatic era in which the conception of truth as agreement with an altogether extra-mental reality was inevitable.

Nevertheless, though on the metaphysical side Leibniz stays with the dogmatists in his acceptance of an *an sich* reality as the ultimate metaphysical basis of truth, still, on the *epistemological* side, he very definitely foreshadows Kant. Consider the following passage, again from the important little essay *De modo distinguendi phaenomena realia ab imaginariis:*

> We must admit it to be true that the criteria for real phenomena thus far offered, even when taken together, are not demonstrative, even though they have the greatest probability; or to speak popularly, that they provide a moral certainty but do not establish a metaphysical certainty, so that to affirm the contrary would involve a contradiction. Thus by no argument can it be demonstrated absolutely that bodies exist, nor is there anything to prevent certain well-ordered dreams from being the objects of our mind, which we judge to be true and which, because of their accord with each other, are equivalent to truth so far as practice is concerned. Nor is the argument which is popularly offered, that this makes God a deceiver, of great importance. ... For what if our nature happened to be incapable of real phenomena? Then indeed God ought not so much to be blamed as to be thanked, for since these phenomena could not be real, God would, by causing them at least to be in [mutual] agreement, be providing us with something equally as valuable in all the practice of life as would be real phenomena. What if this whole short life, indeed, were only some long dream and we should awake at death, as the Platonists seem to think? ... Indeed, even if this whole life were said to be only a dream, and the visible world only a phantasm, I should

call this dream or this phantasm real enough if we were never deceived by it when we make good use of reason. But just as we know from these marks which phenomena should be seen as real, so we also conclude, on the contrary, that any phenomena which conflict with those that we judge to be real, and likewise those whose fallacy we can understand from their causes, are merely apparent.[34]

The lesson of this passage is clear. In the epistemology of perception we have no need for the correspondentist conception of truth as *adaequatio ad rem*. The distinction between appearance and reality is indeed crucial, but it is *for us* a distinction strictly to be drawn *wholly within* the domain of phenomenal reality, and is not a distinction between phenomenal reality on the one hand and noumenal reality on the other.

Thus, while from the God's-eye perspective of his metaphysics Leibniz remains the author of the "system of the Monadology," from the man's-eye perspective of epistemology Leibniz is very much the colleague not only of Kant himself but also of the latter-day idealist supporters of the coherence criteriology of truth.

NOTES

1. Loemker, p. 264.
2. Truths of fact, unlike truths of reason, thus have an essential existential component to the effect that the substances of this possible world are the ones that actually exist. The necessary eternal truths, insofar as they deal with items of contingent existence at all, deal with them in a strictly hypothetical way (see *Nouv. Ess.*, Bk. IV, chap. 11, §13). "Caesar crossed the Rubicon" typifies one case, "If Caesar crossed the Rubicon, then a man crossed a river" typifies the other.
3. PNG §4; *Phil.*, VI, p. 600.
4. Leibniz speaks of the *internal sense* "which may be called reflection; but this reflection is not limited to perceiving the mere operations of the mind, as is stated by Locke; it extends even to perceiving the mind itself ..." (*Phil.*, V. p. 23). Cf. *Nouv, Ess.*, Bk. II, chap. 1, §19.
5. E.g., Latta, *op. cit.*, pp. 34, 121. There is some justification for this, since in §15 of the *Monadology*, Leibniz somewhat carelessly speaks simply of "apperception or consciousness." But of course *or* is sometimes used in the sense of *and* ("Doctors or lawyers may join").
6. Loemker, p. 291.
7. *Nouv. Ess.*, Bk. I, chap. 1, §§19–20.
8. *Nouv. Ess.*, Bk. I, chap. 1, §§2, 27.
9. The standard Leibnizian view is that the innate ideas cover the range of necessary truths, not only in logic and mathematics, but also in metaphysics. Thus, for example, in *New Essays*, Bk. II, Chap. i, §8, Leibniz' spokesman lists as innate ideas such "notions which the senses cannot give" as being, substance, unity, identity, cause, perception, and reason. Yet at an earlier stage of the discussion (Bk. I, Chap. i, §24) Leibniz had, clearly by way of a slip, confined the range to mathematics (in fact, arithmetic and geometry).
10. B. Russell, *Critical Exposition*, p. 163.

11. See especially the important epistle (to Queen Charlotte of Prussia) "On What is Independent of the Senses and of Matter" (*Phil.*, VI., pp. 491–508, tr. only in part in Loemker, pp. 547–8).

12. *Phil.*, VII, p. 529; *Monadology*, §19.

13. It is just this he has in mind when he writes to Arnauld, in a most misleading formulation, that "I reduce all mechanics to a single metaphysical principle" (*Phil.*, II, p. 62; Loemker, p. 338).

14. L.J. Cohen, "On the Project of a Universal Character," *Mind*, vol. 63 (1954), pp. 49–63.

15. See L. Couturat, *La logique de Leibniz* (Paris: Felix Alcan, 1901).

16. *Phil.*, IV, pp. 27–102. This work, written in 1665 and published in the following year, was Leibniz' first substantial philosophical essay. Only some excerpts are tr. in Loemker, pp. 23–92.

17. *Phil.*, VII, p. 192; Loemker, p. 184.

18. *Phil.*, IV, p. 356; Loemker, p. 384.

19. *Phil.*, V, p. 148; *New Essays*, Bk. II, Chap. xix, §4.

20. We return here to the Leibnizian leitmotiv of continuity, already touched upon in Chap. Four.

21. *Nouv. Ess.*, Preface.

22. *Monadology*, §20.

23. *De anima*, 407–10 ff.

24. *Nouv. Ess.*, Bk. II, chap. 1, §19.

25. Loemker, p. 283.

26. *Phil.*, IV, pp. 161–2; Loemker, pp. 129–30.

27. Loemker, p. 283.

28. *Phil.*, I, pp. 195–6; Loemker, p. 188.

29. *Phil.*, VII, pp. 319–20; Loemker, pp. 363–4.

30. *Phil.*, VII, p. 329; Loemker, p. 364.

31. *Ibid.*

32. For a fuller discussion, including references, see N. Rescher, *The Coherence Theory of Truth* (Oxford, 1973).

33. F.H. Bradley, "On Truth and Coherence" in *Essays on Truth and Reality* (Oxford, 1914), pp. 202–218 (see pp. 202–3).

34. Tr. L.E. Loemker, *op. cit.*, pp. 364–5.

Chapter XIII

Moral Philosophy

1. *The Good Life*

The Lockean spokesman in the *New Essays* (Philaletes) is made to voice the ancient Sophists' view that moral principles are not natural (*phusei*, by nature), but man-made (*thesei*, by convention):

> Moral good and moral evil is the conformity or the opposition which is found between voluntary acts and a certain law which brings us (physical) good and evil by the will and power of the lawgiver. ... [1]

Against this background that Leibniz' spokesman (Theophilus) develops his position:

> The previous view not being the ordinary sense that is given to morally good and virtuous acts, I prefer for myself, to take as the measure of moral good and of virtue the invariable rule of reason which God is charged with maintaining. [2]

A right will—specifically including even God's own will—is subject to objective and nonarbitrary moral standards. [3]

The good life—the moral life—is one lived in accordance with "the invariable rule of reason," and the principles of action and justice are codified in two sorts of laws: the divine law (natural and positive) and the civil law (always positive). The social relativity—variability from group to group—of all positive law is recognized, but discounted on the grounds that mistakes are here, as elsewhere, possible:

> Although you [Philaletes] admit that men claim to speak of that which is naturally virtuous or vicious according to immutable laws, you maintain that in fact they mean to speak only of that which depends on opinion. But it seems to me that by the same reasoning you could further maintain that truth and reason and all that could be named as most real, depends on your opinion, because men are mistaken when they judge of it. Is it not better then on all accounts to say, that men understand by virtue as by truth, that which is conformed to nature, but that they are often mistaken in its application; and besides they are mistaken less than they think. [4]

This conception of morality as *action in consonance with general principles of conduct that are conformed to nature* endows Leibniz' ethics with a legalistic cast that reflects not only his own legal training, but also his mathematician's penchant for an orderly system of general principles, and his susceptibility to the influences of Catholic theology.

"Evil," writes Leibniz, "may be taken metaphysically, physically, and morally. Metaphysical evil consists in simple imperfection, physical evil in suffering, and moral evil in sin."[5] Physical and moral evil go back to, and are forms of, metaphysical evil.

Let us consider more closely moral evil, i.e., *sin*. What, according to Leibniz, is its nature? The answer is forthcoming within the legalistic framework of Leibniz' ethics: *transgression*, violation of "the law," especially knowing and calculated transgression. The root source of morals and politics is the disinterested love of others, based on recognition of their intrinsic merit. This, according to Leibniz, generates *natural right* in its three degrees: "*strict right* (*jus strictus*) in commutative justice, *equity*—i.e., *charity* in the narrower sense—in distributive justice, and *piety* (or probity) in universal justice."[6] These varieties of justice define the precincts of law, both positive and moral, and highlight the intimate linkage between them.

Obedience to the law is easier and more certain when we know exactly what the law states—what it in fact requires. This brings up the question of the nature and source of the rules of right action which codify the principles of conduct that are definitive of the good life.

2. *Universal Justice and True Wisdom*

In Leibniz' ethical fragments,[7] which largely occupy themselves with clarification of the key concepts, a trilogy of definitions recurs time and again:[8]

Wisdom is the science of happiness.
Virtue is the habit of acting in accord with wisdom.
Justice is the charity of the wise man, i.e., that which is congruent with the will of the good and prudent man.

The basic convention here is that of human happiness (félicité, bonheur, *felicitas*) defined as "a durable state of pleasure" ("un Estat durable de plaisir," *status laetitiae duraturae*).[9] Pleasure is the starting-point, for:

... the impulse to action arises from a striving toward perfection, the sense of which is pleasure, and there is no action or will on any other basis. Even in our evil purposes we are moved by a certain perceived appearance of good or perfection, even though we miss the mark, or rather pay for a lesser good, ill sought, by throwing away a greater. Nor can anyone renounce (except merely verbally) being impelled by his own good, without renouncing his own nature.[10]

Wisdom is called upon the scene because morally relevant action is always guided by thought; man acts as he *sees fit* to act. Errors of action derive from errors of understanding, much as with Descartes. There are, basically, two sorts of human freedom: freedom of the will *to do what seems best*, and freedom of the understanding to pursue its inquiries *to get clear* on the issues. The will should not be permitted to stray beyond the limits of proper understanding, and lead us into action before the understanding has thoroughly canvassed the relevant considerations:

> It is therefore incumbent on the soul to be on its guard against misleading appearances, and by a firm resolve to reflect and only to act or judge in certain circumstances after mature deliberation.[11]

Haste and heedless enthusiasm must be avoided at all costs. Tayllerand's maxim *Pas trop de zèle* could have originated with Leibniz: wisdom teaches us the proper course of its pursuit. Virtue is the habit of acting wisely; justice is the "charity" of the wise man who puts the happiness of others on a par with his own. The good and just man chooses his actions to conform with the general good.[12] There should be no divergence here, because "... the happiness of those whose happiness pleases us is obviously built into our own, since things which please us are desired for their own sake."[13]

It thus transpires that:

> There is a twofold reason for desiring the good of others: one *is* for our own good, the other *as if* for our own good. ... But, you ask, how it is possible that the good of others should be the same as our own and yet be sought for its own sake? For otherwise the good of others can be our own good only as a means, not as an end. I reply on the contrary that it is also an end, something sought for its own sake, since it is pleasant.[14]

The good act is that which makes for the public good; ethics and politics coalesce.[15] Leibniz' ethic is of that strictly proto-utilitarian character which anticipates the characteristic posture of the Age of Reason. Despite its apparently theocentric origins, it is wholly secular in orientation. To be sure, the good man must "do God's will," but since this will places prime value upon the well-being of that community of spirits whose head is God Himself, it is inevitably God's will that man should act for the benefit of his fellows.

Leibniz harks back to the Greeks, and anticipates the

utilitarians, in the pivotal role his ethical theory accords to *knowledge*. Moral goodness is not a matter of faith, inspiration, or good will, but of *right action*, defined as action that makes for the benefit of the human community. But this is patently a matter of knowledge. The person who can best help an injured man is not just the man of good will but the trained physician, so the person who can best act for the interest of his fellow men is he whose knowledge of the nature of man and of his natural environment can effectively guide his deliberations for action. The pursuit of knowledge itself becomes a major imperative in ethics; wisdom and goodness are joined by an unbreakable bond:

> There are people today who consider it clever to declaim against reason. ... [But] if those who mock at reason spoke in earnest, it would be a new kind of extravagance unknown to past centuries. To speak against reason ... is to speak against one's self, against one's own good, since the principle point of reason consists in knowing the truth and following the good.[16]

In his emphatic stress on reason, Leibniz is a child of his century and a colleague of Spinoza, as in the strikingly Spinozistic passage:

> ... since the power peculiar to the mind is understanding, it follows that we will be the happier the clearer our comprehension of things and the more we act in accordance with our proper nature, namely reason. Only to the extent that our reasonings are correct are we free and exempt from the passions which are impressed upon us by surrounding bodies.[17]

3. *Moral Reasoning and Moral "Instinct"*

Ethics, according to Leibniz, cannot be framed in the strict pattern of a demonstrative science because there are no self-evident (i.e., *analytically* true) truths of reason that could serve as its axiomatic first principles.

> And, although you can truly say that ethics has principles which are not demonstrable, and that one of the first and most practical is, that we ought to pursue joy and avoid sorrow, it is needful to add that this is not a truth which is known purely by reason, since it is based upon internal experience. ...[18]

Certain rules of morality are, however, fundamental, including pre-eminently these two:

> 1. The egocentric hedonic principle that man "ought to pursue joy and avoid sorrow."
> 2. The social principle of the golden rule which is the foundation of all rules of justice: *Do to another only what you would have him do to yourself.*

Knowledge of these rules is arrived at by insight or intuition, and their acceptance is underwritten by instinct. These basic moral rules are innate in that they are not based on external experience, but are an internal drawing on the resources of our own minds. By applying the basic rules, other subordinate rules can be derived by strict reasoning, and thus a (deductive) science of morality is possible. Practical reasoning in situations involving choice (volition) can be carried on by the application of the system of practical principles. Most men, however, do not act on the basis of moral reasoning, but by instinct:

> As morality ... is more important than arithmetic, God has given to man *instincts* which prompt at once and without reasoning to some portion of that which reason ordains; just as we walk in obedience to the laws of mechanics without thinking of these laws. ... But these instincts do not prompt to action in an invincible way; the passions may resist them, prejudices may obscure them, and contrary customs alter them. Nevertheless, we agree most frequently with these instincts of conscience, and we follow them also when stronger impressions do not overcome them.[19]

What for the truly wise man is knowable through "moral science"—intuitive insight into basic principles and subordinate maxims derivable by practical reasonings therefrom—is by the grace of God made accessible to most men through instinct. Despite emphasis on reason, this recourse to instinct makes ample room for unthinking goodness and *fides rustica*. In Leibniz' view the highest forms of virtue are perhaps the private preserve of the highest human intellects, but the elemental requisites for the good life lie within the reach of all.

The greatest felicity within man, however, is to enter under the guidance of reason into the profound truths of mystical theology, thus to sense and respond to the Love of God. This love, the highest possible attainment of the human soul, is a sure consequence of the progress of true knowledge of nature and metaphysics.[20] Man's reason is his main road to true happiness, thus man's natural instinct to seek pleasure and avoid pain will lead him, following the direction of reason, to the highest happiness he can attain. This is why "Wisdom is nothing but the science of happiness itself."[21]

4. *Man's Action and God's Perfection*

Critics of Leibniz have long fixed on two questions as loci of special difficulty for him. Given that God's creation-choice of a particular spirit is made in terms of its complete individual notion that includes every detail of its entire history: (1) How can we speak of "voluntary action" or "free will" at all? (2) How can we impute moral coloration (as praiseworthy or blameworthy, right or wrong) to a substance whose very existence, and consequently capacity to act, is a matter the responsibility for which rests, not with that substance itself, but with God?

The first question is more easily dealt with, for voluntary action is a mode of action, and the general strategy by which Leibniz finds a place for activity within his strictly deterministic scheme can be made to do the necessary work here. A substance acts, according to Leibniz, when it initiates a change of subsequent modifications. It acts "freely" when the substance at issue is a spirit. Its action is the result[22] of inner spontaneity, of a course of rational deliberation as to the eligibility of alternatives, i.e., a deliberate choice among alternates in a manner that includes comparative assessment of their respective goodness. Voluntary action and the exercise of free will are thus matters entirely within the defining individual notion of a substance, and have nothing to do with the fact that the existence of the substance depends upon the acts of God. It is in this sense that voluntary acts, albeit *determined*, are not *necessitated*, and that acts of will—like the events in he causal fabric of nature—have their sufficient reasons, which "incline without necessitating." Human freedom does not oppose predetermination or determination as such.

The decision of the will is always a matter of preferential inclination: there can be no "freedom of indifference" of a will capable of resolving a choice between equally balanced and appealing alternatives. Yet our decision, though invariably *determined*, is exempt from constraint and from necessity,[23] for free action is a matter of the self-determining spontaneity of the spirits: the "inner necessity" of their *own* natures, resulting in acts that are their own, and in no way imposed or constrained. Insofar as a "freely done action" is a meaningful conception, it can figure in the defining (complete) individual notion of a person—he simply conceptualized as "the person who (*inter alia*) freely does X." Once thus conceptualized, he must, of course, necessarily do X, but with a necessity that is wholly hypothetical (*ex hypothesi*) and nowise fatalistic, since the freedom at issue is every bit as operative as the doing of X. (Cf. DM, §30.)

For Leibniz, as for Aristotle, human freedom is the product of deliberation, judgment, and choice, whose authenticity is undisturbed by divine foreknowledge: if a future event is foreseen by the Creator, this does not mean that it will occur *because* it has been predicted by him. Nor is the fact that the complete individual notion or law of the individual series of a substance fixes all its properties and determines all events that will befall it constitute a block to its freedom, since this sort of determination is, according to Leibniz, to be viewed as a mode of self-determination, and thus exemplifies rather than impedes freedom.

Considering Leibniz' response to the first question, his way of dealing with the second becomes more perspicuous and plausible. The pivotal fact is that God does not make a substance what it is; indeed, *God is in no way responsible for what substances do.* When at first (so to speak) the substance subsists merely *sub ratione possibilitatis,* it is in God's mind simply as a conceptualized possibility over which He has no control;[24] He in no way determines the *essence* (nature) of an individual, although he invariably decides its *existence.* Even the best possible world will contain some imperfect substances—some grossly sinful men, for example. Their imperfection is embodied in their intrinsic nature (their complete individual notion), with whose make-up God has nothing to do. What He does have to do with—and this is the *only* aspect of the substance over which He exercises control—is the *existence* of the substance. And He has to confront this choice on *systematic* grounds, between entire possible worlds, and not with respect to the merits or demerits of particular possible substances viewed in isolation. Owing to the interconnectedness of its substances a world must be chosen (or rejected) *en bloc.* God—like the rest of us—has no alternative but to "take the bad with the good." Thus Leibniz writes:

> I have shown that the ancients called Adam's fall Felix Culpa, a happy sin, because it had been retrieved with immense advantage by the incarnation of the Son of God, who has given to the universe something nobler than anything that ever would have been among creatures except for it.[25]

Against this background it becomes possible to appreciate Leibniz' exculpation of God from blame for evil and imperfection as they seem to exist in the world. God bears no responsibility for specific defects of the actual world over which he exercises absolutely no control, and avoids any imputation of imposing necessities upon the world:

> Nor does the foreknowledge or preordination of God impose necessity

even though it is also infallible. For God has seen things in an ideal series of possibles, such as they were to be, and among them man freely sinning. By seeing the existence of this series He did not change the nature of the thing, nor did He make what was contingent necessary.[26]

Each substance has always subsisted (or, strictly speaking, has had being outside of time altogether) *sub ratione possibilitatis* in the mind of God. Its total nature was determined, for its adequate and complete notion (i.e., all of its predicates save existence) was fixed.[27] God bears no responsibility for this nature; it is an object of his understanding, and no creature of his will. God chose for actualization the best, i.e., most perfect, system of compossible substances; He is the reason for all existence, hence for all existent perfection and imperfection. Imperfection is not avoidable since, by the identity of indiscernibles, no substance different from God can be wholly perfect. God, however, chose to minimize imperfection (or, positively, to maximize perfection), thus He is positively the cause of existent perfection, but only negatively of imperfection, since He retained only what could not but remain.

Leibniz distinguishes[28] three modes of evil: *physical* evil, which consists of suffering, *moral* evil, sin, and *metaphysical* evil, the imperfection of creatures. The first two reduce to the third, for if God admits evil into creation, to create it as such would contravene God's own perfection. Evil of any sort cannot properly be said to be *created* by God;[29] rather it is *admitted into existence* by him as an unavoidable concomitant of the perfections he seeks to realize in creation. God has no choice but to tolerate the evils that are an inevitable consequence of the good that is the primary object of his will; He

> ... is willing to permit them unavoidable evils for a greater good. ... This is a *consequent* will, resulting from acts of *antecedent* will, in which one wills the good.[30]

Bertrand Russell has bitterly criticized Leibniz' ethical writings as being full of

> discreditable subterfuges to conceal the fact that *all* sin, for Leibniz, is original sin, the inherent finitude of any created monad. ...[31]

The criticism is unjustified and unjust—there is no concealment at work. What Leibniz wants to show, here as elsewhere, is that the technicalities of his system permit the standard distinctions to be drawn and the standard positions to be taken up. Just as reference to causal action and reaction can be accommodated in a world of windowless monads, the distinction between morality and immorality can be applied *within* the framework of agents totally pre-programmed by their defining individual notions. Leibniz is not attempting to conceal an alien ethic behind a surface of moral platitudes, but to show that an admittedly foreign and unaccustomed perspective can rationally accommodate and account for certain standard traditional views which he and his readers presumably agree in accepting.

NOTES

1. *Nouv. Ess.*, Bk. II, Chap. xxviii, §5.
2. *Nouv. Ess.*, Bk. II, Chap. xxviii, §5.
3. See the important essay, *Reflections on the Common Concept of Justice* in Loemker, pp. 561–73, where the relevant issues are canvassed in substantial detail.
4. *Ibid.*, §10.
5. *Phil.*, VI, p. 115.
6. *Phil.*, III, p. 386 (Loemker, p. 422). From the "Preface to the *Codex Juris Gentium Diplomaticus*" (1693).
7. For these see primarily Gaston Grua, *G.W. Leibniz: Textes inédits*, 2 vols. (Paris: Presses Universitaires de France, 1948).
8. *Ibid.*, Vol. II, pp. 579ff.
9. *Ibid.*, p. 613.
10. *Phil.*, III, p. 389.
11. DM, §30.
12. Note the axiom "Whatever is of public utility is to be done" (*Quicquid publice utile est, faciendum est*), a favourite of Leibniz'.
13. *Phil.*, III, p. 386 (Loemker, pp. 421–2).
14. Loemker, p. 136.
15. See the opuscule entitled *Politica ab ipsa Ethica non est distincta. Ibid.*, p. 563.
16. *Nouv. Ess.*, Bk. II, Chap. xxi, §50.
17. Loemker, p. 281.
18. *Nouv. Ess.*, Bk. I, Chap. ii, §1.
19. *Ibid.*, §9.
20. Grua (ed.), *Textes inédits*, Vol. II, p. 23.
21. *Phil.*, III, p. 386 (Loemker, p. 422).
22. The causal overtones should be suppressed; we mean simply that it is the terminating member of a certain chain of events.
23. "Freedom is as much exempt from *necessity* as from *constraint*. Neither the (determinate) futurity of truths, nor the foreknowledge and pre-ordination of God, nor the predisposition of things creates necessity" (*Causa Dei*, §102; *Phil.*, VI, p. 454).
24. The conceptual possibility simply "is what it is"—nothing (not even itself) "makes it be" that way. The various ethical considerations at issue here are canvassed carefully in the opuscule "Conversation sur la Liberté et sur le Destin" in G. Grua (ed.), *Textes inédits*, pp. 478–86.
25. See the syllogistic abridgment appended to the *Théodicée*. Note, however, that the imperfection of its individual substances does not mean that any *parts* of the best possible world are suboptimal. (Cp. p. 40 above.) The reconciliation here turns to some extent on the part/constituent distinction, for which see pp. 99–104.
26. *Causa Dei*, prop. 104.

27. "The complete or perfect notion of a singular substance involves all its predicates, past, present, and future" (Couturat, *Opuscules*, p. 520; cf. *ibid.*, p. 403). See pp. 15–16 above.

28. *Phil.*, VI, p. 115; *Théodicée*, §21.

29. See *Causa Dei*, §§68–71; *Phil.*, VI, pp. 449–50.

30. *Phil.*, VI, p. 382. *Summary of the Controversy of the "Théodicée" Reduced to Formal Arguments*, Reply to Objection IV.

31. Russell, *Critical Exposition*, p. 197.

Chapter XIV

Theodicy

1. *The Nature and Existence of God*

Our exposition of the philosophy of Leibniz began with a discussion of God and it must end there as well. He is the alpha and omega of the system.

Leibniz repeatedly critized Descartes and Spinoza for relying exclusively on one single argument for God's existence—the refurbished Ontological Argument of St. Anselm. He urged that other proofs, especially arguments that proceed from "the order of things," be used. Even if these wider-ranging reasonings should prove redundant from the exclusively rational point of view, they would prove of great persuasive use in helping to solidify the conviction of the ordinary man and "to silence the Atheist." Leibniz thus gave special prominence to five different arguments: the Ontological Argument, the Cosmological Argument, the Argument from Eternal Truths, the Argument from Design, and the Modal Argument. Let us consider them in turn.[1]

2. *The Ontological Argument*

The Ontological Argument infers God's existence from His perfection. Starting with the definition of God as "the (all-)*perfect* being"—or alternatively as "the *most real* being"—it argues that *existence*, since it is a mode of perfection (or reality), must characterize this particular Being. Leibniz added one important qualification to this classical form of the argument. The line of reasoning involved attempts to elicit the necessity of its conclusion by inference from a premise which is, in effect, a definition. But, said Leibniz, a definition can be self-inconsistent, with the thing it purportedly defines actually impossible; "the fastest motion" and "the largest circle" were examples he gave. The Ontological Argument thus does no more than prove that, if God is possible, he exists. The question of possibility remains to be settled,[2] and represents an additional step needed to render the argument cogent.

Leibniz employed several alternative reasonings to establish the possibility of a Being answering to the definition basic to the Ontological Argument. One takes the following form: the possibility of God follows *a posteriori* from the existence of contingent things. (This argument is developed at greater length below.) A second line of reasoning takes the more orthodox (i.e., traditional) form of maintaining that all modes of perfection are necessarily compatible with one another, so there could be no self-inconsistency in the idea of a Being which exhibits each of them in highest degree. The details of the reasoning are this. A *perfection* is, by definition, a quality that is (1) *simple* of absolute, and thus indefinable, and (2) *positive* and expresses its object without any restrictions or limitations. Two such qualities P and Q cannot possibly conflict when attributed to the same subject; incompatibility could arise only if they differ in direction (positivity or negativity), degree (i.e., extent), or resolutive constituents. But all of these possibilities are excluded by defining a quality as representing a perfection. Of course, if existence is included as a perfection in the sense of this definition, it will have to be classed as a quality, though of a very unusual nature.[3] This is, as Kant was to remark, a major point of weakness in this argument.

3. *The Cosmological Argument (or the Argument from Sufficient Reason)*

The starting point of the Cosmological Argument, as Leibniz formulates it, is not a definition of any sort of necessary premiss, but a contingent fact: the existence of the world. Any particular happening in the world can always be explained in terms of its earlier states and the natural laws that govern its changes, but what of general questions regarding the nature of the world and its laws; why do things occur in the world as they do rather than otherwise? What is at issue is not the reason for any single member of the endless series of specific world states, but the reason for the whole series. Why are there any states at all? Why are they as they are rather than otherwise? Given the (logically necessary) Principle of Sufficient Reason, the whole series of world states must have a supermundane reason that lies outside itself. But the sufficient reason for the sphere of contingence must lie outside the sphere, in the sphere of the metaphysically necessary. Moreover, the reason for an existing thing must itself be an existing thing, thus the sufficient reason for the realm of contingence must be a metaphysically necessary existent—a Being whose essence involves existence—and this can only be God.[4]

Within its Leibnizian framework, the major shortcomings of this argument are twofold. First, it rests upon a purely factual premise—the existence of a range of contingents. This is a mild and venial failing, since the presupposition is not readily denied. The second, more serious, failing has to do with the *manner* in which the argument applies the Principle of Sufficient Reason: even if the applicability of the principle is conceded to Leibniz, his insistence upon locating the reason for the character of contingents in one unique existent external to the domain at issue still represents a questionable procedure.

4. *The Argument from Eternal Truths*

This argument rests on the persupposition (it is no more than that, since Leibniz nowhere argues explicitly for its truth) that the eternal truths must have a locus of existence—that whatever exists must ultimately pertain to a *substance*. Leibniz repeatedly describes God's understanding as the region of the eternal truths.[5] Man's recognition of certain truths as eternal is consequently deemed a sufficient basis for his inference to the existence of a Deity. The supposition seems to be that a truth cannot exist unthought, thus the existence of an eternal truth requires its location in the thought of an eternal thinker.

5. *The Argument from Design*

This ancient argument for the existence of God is based on the analogy of the human workman. As the plan and organization of the building attest to the arrangements of the master architect, so the great subtlety encountered in the works of nature attest the planning mind of the great Creator. The only characteristic touch Leibniz adds to the classic pattern of this reasoning has to do with the pre-established harmony. The endless coordination and mutual accommodation of existing substances cannot be accounted for except as the work of an all-knowing intellect. We can thus argue from the orderliness of the world,[6] and not simply from its existence, as with the Argument from Sufficient Reason, to the existence of a God in whom responsibility for this orderliness lies. The major weakness of the argument lies in its "exclusivity presupposition," to the effect that a certain feature of the universe (viz., its orderliness) is to be accounted for in only one conceivable way (viz., as the work of the Deity).

6. *The Modal Argument*

A further proof of God's existence might well be termed the

Modal Argument: like the Ontological Argument it starts from a definition of God, but establishes His existence not by ordinary but by *modal* reasoning.[7] This characteristically Leibnizian proof of the existence of God is often overlooked. It is, for example, omitted in Russell's discussion, following that of Erdmann, of four such proofs offered by Leibniz—the Anselmio-Cartesian Ontological Argument, the Cosmological Argument, the Argument from Eternal Truths, and the Argument from the Pre-established Harmony.[8]

His theory of definition underlay Leibniz' dissatisfaction with the Anselmio-Cartesian Ontological Argument. This theory rests on the classification of definitions as *real* and *nominal: nominal* if not real, and *real* if the *definiens* is shown to be possible, i.e., consistent.[9] The difficulty with the Ontological Argument, which embarks from the definition of God as *the perfect being*, is that it is open to doubt that such a being is possible, and any maneuvering intended to dispel this doubt by demonstrating the freedom from contradiction of the definition introduces further complexities. It would thus be advantageous to jettison perfection, and to start afresh from a quite different—less problematic—definition of God:

> The Geometers, who are the past masters of the art of reasoning, have realized that in order that proofs based on definitions be valid one must show, or at least postulate, that the notion comprised in any of the definitions used is possible. ... The same precaution is necessary in every type of reasoning, and above all in the demonstration due to Anselm, Archbishop of Canterbury (*in libro contra insipientem*), which proves that since God is the greatest or most perfect being, He possesses also that perfection termed *existence*, and that consequently He exists; an argument which was subjected to scrutiny by Saint Thomas and other Scholastics, and which was revived by M. Descartes. Regarding this it must be said that the argument is quite valid, providing that the supremely perfect being or that which comprises all perfections is possible. Just this is the priviledge of the divine nature—that its essence contains its existence, i.e., that God exists provided only that He is possible. And even omitting all reference to perfection, one can say: *If the Necessary Being is possible, He exists*—doubtless the most beautiful and important proposition of the doctrine of modalities, since it furnishes a passage from possibility to actuality, and it is here and here alone that *a posse ad esse valet consequentia.*[10]

Thus Leibniz establishes the existence of God by defining Him as the *Necessary Being*,[11] and by invoking modal reasoning to show that such a being exists provided only that its existence is possible. It remains for him to demonstrate that the Necessary Being is possible, which he does by adducing another purported theorem of modal logic:

Those who hold that one can never infer actual existence solely from notions, ideas, definitions, or possible essences ... deny the possibility of the Necessary Being. ... But if the Necessary Being or *Ens a se* is impossible, then all of the things which owe their existence to others will be impossible, since they must ultimately stem from the *Ens a se*. Thus no existence at all will be possible. ... This reasoning leads us to another modal proposition ... which joined with the previous one (*If the Necessary Being is possible, then He exists*) completes the demonstration. This proposition can be formulated thus: *If the Necessary Being does not exist, neither will anything else.*[12]

It appears that the entire argument takes the following form:

1. If the Necessary Being is not possible, then no existence is possible.
2. If the Necessary Being is possible, then He exists.
3. Therefore, if the Necessary Being does not exist, then nothing exists.
4. But something exists.
5. Hence the Necessary Being exists.[13]

This Modal Argument is Leibniz' preferred demonstration for the existence of God.

7. *God's Metaphysical and Moral Perfection Differ in Necessity*

We have seen that the perfection of a substance is the same as its quantity of essence, which determines its potentiality for existence. As Leibniz sees it, this circumstance underlies God's manner of proceeding in making a creation choice. (See pp. 33–34.) But the transition from perfection to quantity of essence to existence also operates with respect to God Himself, as the Ontological Argument shows. And now a serious difficulty arises. For if the existence of God—i.e. a being of God's characteristic nature and essence—is necessary, and God's *modus operandi* in his creation choice is also necessary, then does this not mean that a Spinozistic necessity also constrains the existence of the world as we have it? How is any room left for contingency in the scheme of things?

Leibniz proposes to resolve this difficulty by inserting the wedge of a sharp distinction between God's *nature* (and thus His *existence*, which follows from it) on the one hand, and His *actions* (and thus His creation choice) on the other. The distinction at issue turns on that between God's *metaphysical* perfection and His *moral* perfection. Let us see how this distinction works.

Since God exists necessarily in consequence of his own nature, His existence being contained in His essence, it follows that God has the highest possible degree of perfection. And so God is not only the *necessary*, but also, in consequence, the *perfect* being. But at this point we must draw attention to an equivocation in Leibniz' word "perfection," an equivocation of which he himself was perfectly well aware. There is firstly "perfection" as a measure of potentiality for existence, which we have already considered, and secondly "perfection" as a moral attribute, goodness. Leibniz terms the former *metaphysical*, the latter *moral* perfection, and he insists that these must be discriminated.[14] God is, however, perfect in both senses; as "the necessary being" He possesses the maximum amount of essence (=metaphysical perfection), and as maxi-benevolent being His acts (the sphere of His activity being the world) are the best possible (whence moral perfection). But while God's existence, hence His metaphysical perfection, is necessary, His goodness as creator, i.e., moral perfection, is contingent and the result of free choice. "The true reason why these things rather than those exist is to be attributed to the free decrees of the divine will, the first and foremost of which is to act in all respects in the most perfect possible way, as befits the wisest of being."[15]

Leibniz accordingly divides God's characteristics into those which are free (contingent) and those which are necessary:[16]

From this, then, it becomes clear that the acts of God must be distinguished into the free and the necessitated. Thus, that God loves Himself is necessary, for it follows from the definition of *God*. But that God chooses the most perfect cannot be so demonstrated, for its denial implies no contradiction.[17]

And again,

One can say in a certain sense that it is necessary ... that God Himself choose what is best. ... But *this* necessity is not at all at odds with contingence, it not being that necessary which I call logical, geometric, or metaphysical, whose denial is contradictory.[18]

It remains to clarify the relation between God's necessary metaphysical and His contingent moral perfection. In order to do this we must once more call to mind Leibniz' Principle of Sufficient Reason. As we have seen, this asserts that every true proposition can be shown to be analytic by a (possibly infinite) process of "analysis" of "demonstration," i.e., a successive elimination of defined ideas by means of their definition. Using this principle, we can clarify the logical relation between the two types of divine perfection. God's moral perfection (goodness) has a sufficient reason, and this in turn another, *et cetera ad infinitum;* but this sequence of sufficient reasons converges on God's metaphysical perfection.[19] Or, putting this another way, we can say that God's moral perfection is indeed an inevitable consequence of His nature—of His metaphysical perfection—but a consequence which no finite deduction suffices to elicit. It follows, but not finitely; it is necessary but only *morally* necessary and not metaphysically so—i.e., in a sense that precludes contingence.[20] In this way, as Leibniz insists, the proposition asserting God's moral perfection is necessitated, but indicated by an infinite series of choice—involving steps.[21] As usual, it is precisely the presence of an infinite regress (which Russell invokes in his *reductio ad absurdum* of Leibniz' contention that God's goodness is contingent) which establishes this contingence, since *radix contingentiae est in infinitum.*

But while God's existence, and hence His metaphysical perfection, is, as we have seen, necessary, His goodness as creator, i.e., moral perfection, is contingent and the result of free choice. "The true reason why these things rather than those exist is to be attributed to the free decrees of the divine will, the first and foremost of which is to act in all respects in the most perfect possible way, as befits the wisest of beings."[22] God's moral perfection (goodness) has a sufficient reason, and this in turn another, *et caetera ad infinitum*; but this sequence of sufficient reasons converges on God's metaphysical perfection.[23] Or, putting this another way, we can say that God's moral perfection is indeed a logical consequence of His metaphysical perfection, but a consequence which no finite deduction can ever encompass. As Leibniz put the issue:

> If anyone asks me why God has to decide to create Adam, I say, because he has decided to do the most perfect thing. If you ask me now why he had decided to do the most perfect thing, or why he wills the most perfect ... I reply that he has willed it feely, i.e., because he willed to. So he willed because he willed to will, and so on to infinity.[24]

In this way, as Leibniz insists, the proposition asserting God's moral perfection is contingent; God is good by free choice, not necessitation.

Thus Leibniz would deal with the dilemma with which we initially presented him by accepting, and indeed insisting on the truth of, the second horn. Infinite processes can be accomplished by God in a way comprehensible to us only analogically, by means of infinite series and the calculus.

The Principle of Perfection, being a contingent truth,[25] *must* itself involve an infinite regress of sufficient reason.[26] Analysis of the contingent must lead to the necessary, i.e., to God *qua* metaphysically perfect.[27] Hence God's moral perfection must be grounded in His metaphysical perfection, but the derivation of the former from the latter requires an infinity of steps. It is by means of *the infinite* that Leibniz reconciles God's freedom and perfection with the Principle of Sufficient Reason,[28] and this problem of reconciliation, instead of being the weak spot of Leibniz' philosophy, provides the key to its inner sanctum—the infinitistic character of the contingent: *Contingentiae radix est in infinitum* ("The ground of contingency is in the infinite").

Until the middle 1680's, when his mature philosophy took form, Leibniz held a different view, as some brief tracts recently published by Grua reveal. He held that God's acts are *both* necessary and free.

> Since GOD necessarily and yet freely chooses the most perfect, whenever there is one thing better than another, it follows that His freedom is always preserved [in choices] although there never existed and never could exist a case in which there is no reason for choosing one of two equally perfect [essences][29]

God's choice of the best is necessary, but what is to result from that choice is not, for it is not determined with necessity which of the alternatives is the best.

> Though it is true that it is necessary that God choose the best, still it does not follow that the best is necessary or that which He chooses is necessary, for it is not determined with necessity what is best.[30]

Thus when H.W.B. Joseph writes, "What I should like myself to suggest by way of conclusion is, that the acts of God perhaps ought to have been declared free, but not contingent ..."[31] he suggests to Leibniz a position he did, at an early point in his career, hold. But it is not surprising that Leibniz abandoned this position, for it is difficult to see how what is best could avoid being determined with necessitation when the substances are conceived *sub ratione possibilitatis*. So we later find Leibniz flatly identifying liberty with "contingence or non-necessity."[32]

8. *The City of God*

The monads of the highest grade, the spirits, alone share with God in both the intellectual capacity for self-consciousness and the moral capacity for reasoned choice based on a vision of the good. Whereas all monads mirror the created world of other monads, the spirits are a reflection, albeit a pale one, of God as well. The spirits comprise the City of God:

> ... this truly universal monarchy, [which] is a moral world within the natural world, and [is] the highest and most divine of the works of God. It is in this [sphere] that the glory of God truly consists, for He would have none of His greatness and goodness, were they not admired by spirits. It is, too, in relation to this divine city that He properly has goodness: whereas His wisdom and power are manifest everywhere.[33]

The spirits alone are capable of self-consciousness (*apperception*), and thus they alone can perceive the moral coloration of their own actions as right or wrong. As the sole created existent capable of conscious choice and intelligent action, a spirit "imitates, in its own province and in the little world in which it is allowed to act, what God does in the great World."[34] Human life in its ethical, cultural, and aesthetic perspective is a separate dimension of the physical and organic realm, a "moral world within the natural world." Forming the population of the City of God, over which He is the monarch, the spirits owe each other that mutuality of common concern that reflects in miniature God's prime concern for the welfare of the spirits in his creative choice of the best possible universe. The goal of Leibniz' social philosophy is the creation of a universal society which mirrors the great Kingdom of spirits, of which God is the head. (This ethical motive seems to be one of the main reasons for Leibniz' insistence upon the omnitemporality of spirits, i.e., the fact of their co-eternality with the world.[35])

Though ethics can stand on its own foundation, it nevertheless points towards theology: in action, as in knowledge, God provides the ultimate, infinitely removed, ideal. This ideal is one which the moral man should, and the family of spirits on the whole does, hold constantly in view, the free activity of the spirits is aimed at and works towards it. We live and act in the image of God—in the small sphere of our own free actions we too are creative agents and in the cognitive sphere we too can penetrate the domain of eternal truths. Here we have Leibniz' vision of the great purposive scheme of creation: universal progress toward perfection, directed toward a *telos* that is ever goal but never destination—movement without arrival, improvement without perfection.

In his projects for advancing the sciences and his promotion of learned academies and institutions, Leibniz strove to implement his own ethical commitments according to his best abilities. For him, reunion of the churches, for example, was a pre-eminently feasible and *moral* goal: since truth is one, and human spirits are citizens of the City of God, one theological system should be able to unite the religious principles of all right-thinking men. (Think here of Nicholas of Cusa's motto of *una religio in rituum varietate*.)

In good action, the example of God, the will of God, and the welfare of one's fellows come together in an indissoluble unity. Leibniz writes:

> The good is that which by the general institution of God is conformed to [i.e., rendered conformable by] nature or reason.[36]

Since God's goodness is embodied in nature, His creation, we can learn the principles of ethics—the canons of human welfare—from scientific study of the rational structure of His *modus operandi* in this sphere. The scientific study of nature not only points the way toward the good life, but also puts into our hands the tools by which the prime aim of ethics, the advancement of human welfare, can be achieved. For Leibniz, all ethically sound human action is oriented toward working out the great design of creation—realization of God's kingdom in this world. The unity of God's plan and of the ethical scheme is one of the constitutive harmonies definitive of the best possible world.

9. *The Primacy of Spirits*

The welfare of the spirits is, as discussed already, a prime consideration with God: "There is no room for doubt that the felicity of the spirits is the principle aim of God and that He puts this purpose into execution as far as the general harmony will permit."[37] But even God cannot exclude the moral evil of spirits from the best possible world (this is the root of original sin for Leibniz), for God has no control over an evil that inheres in the definitive nature of a spirit. Hence:

> The grace of God, whether ordinary or extraordinary, has its degrees and its measures. It is always of itself ... sufficient not only to keep one from sin but even to effect his salvation, provided that a man does his part in cooperating with it. It [i.e., God's grace] has not always, however, sufficient power to overcome a man's inclination, for if it did it would no longer be limited in any way. ...[38]

His eagerness to assign a special status to spirits within the realm of monads leads Leibniz into some of the more remote reaches of his system. Every monad has its continuing historical self-identity, as codified in its complete individual notion and concretized in its present reflection of its past states. But spirits exhibit not only the continuing metaphysical self-identity of all created substances but also a moral self-identity. Cosmic history is so arranged that a spirit never descends to the level of a bare monad; it always has a body, i.e., is the dominant monad of an organically structured aggregate. No matter how low this may descend on the organic scale, a spirit always, throughout its whole history, qualifies for membership in the community of morally qualified individuals.

God performs miracles especially for the sake of the spirits over whom he presides as monarch. Leibniz explains in his correspondence with Clarke that a "miracle" is any act which, like the creation itself, "surpasses the powers of creatures."[39] The acts of divine choice aimed to assure the benefit of the spirits are miraculous, but that does not make them arbitrary or inexplicable:

> As God can do nothing without reasons, even when He acts miraculously, if follows that He has no will about individual events but what results from some general truth or will. This I would say that God never has a *particular will* ... i.e., a *particular primitive will.* I think even that miracles have nothing to distinguish them from other events in this regard: for reasons of an order superior to that of Nature [i.e., the "common course of nature"] prompt God to perform them.[40]

10. *A Point of Difficulty*

His commitments to the conception of the "City of God," with its corresponding emphasis upon the welfare of the "spirits"—the highest grade of substances represented by intelligent, mind-endowed beings—betrayed Leibniz into one of the noteworthy discrepancies of his system. He is, as we have seen, fundamentally committed to the criterion of a "best possible" world as one that exhibits "the simplest laws with the richest phenomena." This highly metaphysical conception of goodness stands in potential conflict with a more emphatically moral criterion, acknowledging God's primary responsibility to the spirits.[41] In one particularly important discussion, however, Leibniz makes it clear that he is prepared to see the metaphysical considerations prevail over the ethical ones, in the final analysis:

> [Objection] "*If there is more evil than good in intelligent creatures, there is more evil than good in all God's work?*" [Reply] ... I do not admit it because this supposed inference from the part to the whole, from intelligent creatures to all creatures, assumes tacitly and without proof that creatures devoid of reason cannot be compared or taken into account with those that have reason. But why might not the surplus of good in the nonintelligent creatures that fill the world compensate for

and even exceed incomparably the surplus of evil in rational creatures? It is true that the value of the latter is greater; but by way of compensation the others are incomparably greater in number; and it may be that the proportion of number and quantity surpasses that of value and quality.[42]

To the extent that this passage is regarded as representing Leibniz' considered and mature position—and I think that in the final analysis it probably should be so taken—it must be regarded as a triumph of the cold-blooded metaphysician over the moral philosopher and the Christian theologian.

This gap—or rather this tension—between God's universally operative *ontological* beneficence and his specifically *moral* benefience is never satisfactorily closed by Leibniz. The idea that this tension is resolvable—and indeed resolved in this "best of all possible worlds"—is, with Leibniz, a fundamental act of philosophic faith, and not a systematic part of his system, let alone a logical exigency of its principles.

Our world—the actual world—is the "best possible world" in this rarified metaphysical sense of *greatest variety of phenomena consonant with greatest simplicity of laws*. Its being the best has (at bottom) little to do with how men (or men and animals) fare in it. The facile optimism of Dr. Pangloss, the butt of Voltaire's parody *Candide—Si c'est ici le meilleur des mondes possibles, que sont donc les autres?*[43]—misses the mark if Leibniz (and not some naive and simple-minded Leibnizian) is intended as its target.

11. *Cosmic Evolution and Melioration*

Leibniz discusses, without committing himself, the possibility of a first instant, prior to all others both in time and in nature. By his own statement this question of a first instant is closely allied with the changes of the state of perfection of the universe:

One may form two hypotheses, the one that nature is always equally perfect, the other that it always grows in perfection. If it [nature] is always equally perfect [as a whole], but variable [in the parts], it is more probable that there was no beginning [of the universe]. But if it always grows in perfection (assuming that it is not possible to give it all its perfection at once) the question may again be explicated in two ways. ...[44]

These two ways are (1) a growth of perfection from all eternity which, since it has not come to an end, must be asymptotic; and (2) an increase of perfection starting from a fixed instant of creation. Leibniz arrives at no final conclusion, and concludes his discussion saying: "I do not yet see a way to show demonstratively which [solution] one ought to choose according to pure reason."[45] In his fifth letter to Clarke, Leibniz writes:

> If the nature of things as a whole is to grow uniformly in perfection, the universe of creatures must have had a beginning.[46] Thus it is more reasonable to postulate a beginning for it than to admit limits for it, in order to secure ... the character of its infinite Author.[47]

But here too Leibniz does not commit himself.[48]

Although Leibniz hesitates, for lack of final proof, to be dogmatic in regard to the quantity of past time or change in the relative perfection of the universe, he personally inclines, with respect to the latter question, toward an increase. Here, as elsewhere, we find a dynamic tendency in Leibniz' thought; he clearly prefers the idea of a developing plan of campaign, a continuing project, to that of an architect's plan, a static picture. His grounds for inclination toward a growth in perfection are in the psychological observation that human happiness lies in the anticipation of greater future goods.[49] It is because in its changes a monad approaches asymptotically a final high point of perfection that the analogy between Leibniz' *appetition* and Spinoza's *conatus* cannot be pressed, as some interpreters have inclined to do. We see here, once again, Leibniz' tendency to insist on metaphysical counterparts to an ethical theme:

> As for the afflictions, especially of good men, however, we must take it as assured that these lead to their greater good and that this is true not only theologically but also naturally. ... In general, one may say that, though afflictions are temporary evils, they are good in effect, for they are shortcuts to greater perfection. ... We may call this backing up the better to spring forward ("qu'on recule pour mieux sauter").[50]

This inclination toward a theory of cosmic melioration is one of the striking characteristics of Leibniz' optimism. It is distinctly a decorative feature added to the basic structure of his philosophy, and not an inexorable consequence of its fundamental positions.

12. *Excursus*

Modern commentators tend to remark disparagingly upon the striking contrast of Leibniz' system between its daringly innovative logic, epistemology, and metaphysics and its extremely conservative ethics and theology. (Similar complaints are sometimes lodged against Descartes.) Bertrand Russell has even suggested that Leibniz had two systems: "the good philosophy which he had kept to himself, and ... the vulgarized version by which he won the admiration of Princes and (even more) of Princesses."[51] This view of the matter is in fact wholly unjustified. Quite the reverse seems true: the guiding aim and aspiration of Leibniz' philosophy is to establish a rigorous rational foundation for what he accepted as the fundamental teachings of ethics and theology. To do this in detail and provide the means for a solid demonstration of "the conformity of faith with reason" took Leibniz into the construction of a highly novel philosophy. But its novelties were not introduced for their own sake. Rather, Leibniz is a thinker who feels himself constrained to use uncommon means to achieve a familiar, commonplace destination. His immensely penetrative intelligence led Leibniz to the construction of a highly unorthodox theory, but he never concealed from himself the fact (which we too must realize) that the purpose of this theory was to provide a conceptually solid underpinning for certain essentially orthodox views in ethics and theology.

It is surprising to what extent Leibniz brought himself to a belief that the orthodox character of his ends could get his readers to accept the unusual route by which he reached them. The correspondence with Arnauld on the nature of substance and that with des Bosses on transubstantiation bear remarkable evidence of this. Leibniz genuinely believed that if an intellectually secure foundation for ethics and theology were provided, men would be brought together. He never abandoned this optimistic goal, not even in the face of endless discouragements.

Leibniz eagerly wanted to persuade his readers (usually his correspondents), not in order to win personal disciples in high places, but to secure effective adherents to implement a vision of truths which he felt capable of healing the theological strifes and political discords in Europe of his day. Had fame been his prime goal he would have written more books and fewer letters. What Leibniz wanted was not public acclaim, but influential converts who could implement in the sphere of action his reconciling insights in the sphere of thought. With Leibniz, self-aggrandizement was never an end in itself, but a means towards a less ignoble end. It is always risky to speculate on motives, but in my own mind there is no doubt that the aspirations which actuated him were, in the main, not those of selfishness but of public spirit.

NOTES

1. An interesting discussion of the historical development of Leibniz' views on proofs for the existence of God—essentially an evolution from early prime reliance upon the Ontological Argument to a late emphasis on what we have called the Modal Argument—can be found in Wolfgang Janke, "Das Ontologische Argument in der Frühzeit des Leibnizchen Denkens (1676–1678)," *Kantstudien*, vol. 54 (1963), pp. 259–87.

2. This objection had already been made to Descartes, and he replied to it in his answers to the second set of objectives to his *Meditations*. See V. Cousin, ed., *Oeuvres de Descartes*, Vol. I, pp. 407, 440 ff.

3. Compare §5 of Chap. II, and cf. footnote 9 of Chap. VIII.

4. *Phil.*, VII, p. 302 (Loemker, p. 486).

5. E.g., *Phil.*, VI, p. 115; VII, p. 311.

6. The argument thus also rests on a factual premise.

7. That the argument we are about to consider was preferred by Leibniz over others which he gave at times, and that it is this argument which he regarded as the most cogent was, to my knowledge, first pointed out by J. Iwanicki (*Leibniz et les démonstrations mathématiques de l'existence de Dieu* [Strasbourg: Librairie Universitaire d'Alsace, 1933], p. 207). Leibniz habitually supplemented his discussions of the Anselmio-Cartesian Ontological Argument by some such appendage as: "But even leaving out all mention of the divine perfection or grandeur, one can formulate the argument thus far in a more proper and rigorous fashion as follows " (*Phil.*, IV, p. 359; Loemker, p. 386). What follows is the Modal Argument.

8. See pp. 172 ff. of Russell's *Critical Exposition*, and cf. J.E. Erdmann, *Geschichte der Philosophie*, II, pp. 168–69.

9. DM, §24.

10. *Ibid.*, pp. 401–2.

11. "Ens a se," "L'Estre de soy," "Ens necessarium," "L'Estre necessaire," "L'Estre qui doit exister parce qu'il est possible."

12. *Phil.*, IV, pp. 359, 406.

13. The second is, so Leibniz would have it, true by definition. If, accordingly, we grant Leibniz the right to assume that 2 holds for "the Necessary Being," then, since 3 follows from 1 and 2, and since we can scarcely cavil at 4, it is clear that the burden is borne here by the (assuredly dubious) premise 1. It should further be remarked that, as Leibniz gives it, the demonstration is an enthymeme, in which the tacit existential premise 4 lurks. Nevertheless, this at worst invalidates the claim that the demonstration of possibility is *a priori*, but does not undermine the existence proof.

14. "And lest any should think of confounding moral perfection or goodness with metaphysical perfection or magnitude (*magnitudine*). ... " it must be remarked that the latter is quantity of essence or reality, while the former arises when metaphysical perfection is the object of a choosing mind (*Phil.*, VII, pp. 305–6; Loemker, p. 489; see also G. Grua, *G.W. Leibniz: Textes inédits* [Paris: Presses Universitaires de France, 1948], I, p. 393). This distinction of Leibniz' has been almost universally overlooked. But if moral and metaphysical perfection are not discriminated, the distinction between moral and metaphysical necessity also collapses, as has been generally charged.

15. *Phil.*, VII, pp. 309–10, notes. On this basis the very *possibility* of "the (morally) perfect being" becomes a moot issue for the argument. Leibniz handles this *via* the principle that *all perfections are compatible with one another*. For the ramifications of these ideas see *Phil.*, VII, pp. 261–2 (tr. in Langley's tr. of the *Nouv. Ess.*, pp. 714–16).

16. Specifically, while the nature and existence of God and His relationships to

various eternalia (Himself included) are all necessary, His choices and creative action vis-à-vis contingent existence is itself contingent. The contingency of mundane existence spills over (by way of presupposition) into a contingent aspect of God himself. As Leibniz sees it, the recognition of a God whose make-up does not exclude relationships with the contingent as a departure from classical Aritotelianism necessitated by the transition to a Christian framework of thought.

17. Grua, *Textes*, I, p. 288.

18. *Phil.*, VI, p. 284.

19. This is so since the (infinite) analysis of the contingent *must* ultimately lead to the necessary, i.e., to God *qua* metaphysically perfect (*Phil.*, VII, p. 200). It is because he holds this that Leibniz, speaking now in the language not of truths but of things, maintains, "If there were no necessary being, there would be no contingent being" (*Phil.*, VII, p. 310).

20. See Grua, *Textes indédites*, p. 393, and cf. p. 276, 288-9.

21. See Grua, *Textes indédites*, p. 302.

22. *Phil.*, VII, 309-310, notes. "From this, then, it becomes clear that the acts of God must be distinguished into the free and the necessitated. Thus, that God loves Himself is necessary, for it follows from the definition of God. But that God chooses the most perfect cannot be so demonstrated, for its denial implies no contradiction" (Grua, *Textes*, I, 288). "One can say in a certain sense that it is necessary ... that God Himself choose what is best. ... But *this* necessity is not at all at odds with contingence, it not being that necessary which I call *logical, geometric*, or *metaphysical*, whose denial is contradictory" (*Phil.*, VI, 284).

Until the year 1685/6, when his mature philosophy took form, Leibniz held a different view, as some brief tracts recently published by Grua reveal. He held that God's acts are both necessary and free. "*Cum DEUS necessario et tamen libere eligat perfectissimum ...*" (Grua, *Textes*, I, 276). God's choice of the best is necessary, but what it to result from that choice is not, for it is not determined with necessity which of the alternatives is the best. "Though it is true that it is necessary that God choose the best, still it does not follow that the best is necessary or that which He chooses is necessary, for it is not determined with necessity what is best" (*ibid.*, I, 305-6). Thus when H.W.B. Joseph writes, "What I should like myself to suggest by way of conclusion is, that the acts of God perhaps ought to have been declared free, but not contingent ..." (*Lectures on the Philosophy of Leibniz*, p. 188), he suggests to Leibniz a position he did, at an early point in his career, hold. But it is not surprising that Leibniz abandoned this position. For it is difficult indeed to see how what is best could avoid being determined with necessitation when the substances are conceived *sub ratione possibilitatis*. And so we find Leibniz later flatly identifying liberty with "contingence or non-necessity" (*Phil.*, VI, 296).

23. This is so since the (infinite) analysis of the contingent *must* ultimately lead to the necessary, i.e., to God qua metaphysically perfect (*Phil.*, VII, 200). It is because he helds this that Leibniz, speaking now in the language not of truths but of things, maintains, "*Si nullum esset Ens necessarium, nullum foret Ens contingens*" (*Phil.*, VII, 310).

24. Grua, *Textes*, I, p. 302.

25. The Principle of Perfection is itself the cardinal and primary contingent truth, for all that exists contingently does so "... by the free decrees of the divine will, of which the primary one is the decision to do everything in the best possible way, as seems wisest" (*Phil.*, VII, pp. 309-10, notes).

26. "A true contingent proposition cannot be reduced to an identity but is nonetheless tested by showing with continued greater and greater resolution that it indeed approaches identity perpetually, but never reaches it" (Couturat, *Opuscules*, p. 388).

27. "But this progression to infinity (of the analysis of truths of fact) has the locus of its cause ... outside the series (of truths of contingence in God ..." (*Phil.*, VII, p. 200). "It is evident from these considerations that the ultimate extraworldly

reason of things, or God, cannot be escaped by means of a postulated eternity of the world," or "The considerations show clearly that we cannot escape an ultimate extramundane reason for things, or God, even by assuming the eternity of the world" (*Phil.*, VII, p. 303; Loemker, pp. 486–7). "If the necessary Being is possible, he exists. For the necessary Being and the Being-by-his-essence are one and the same thing. ... If the Being-through-self is impossible, all beings through others are so too, since they only are, in the end, through the Being-through-self: and thus nothing could exist" (*Phil.*, IV, p. 406). "If there were no necessary being, there would be no contingent being" (*Phil.*, VII, p. 310).

28. "The root cause of contingency is in the infinite: A contingent truth is one which is indemonstrable" (Couturat, *Logique*, p. 212, n. 3).

29. Grua, *Textes*, I, p. 276.

30. *Ibid.*, pp. 305–6.

31. *Lectures on the Philosophy of Leibniz*, p. 188.

32. *Phil.*, VI, p. 296.

33. *Mondalogy*, §86. Cf. PNG, §§14–15.

34. PNG, §14.

35. Cf. *Phil.*, VI, p. 517.

36. *Nouv. Ess.*, Bk. II, Chap. xxviii, §5.

37. DM, §5.

38. DM, §30.

39. *Phil.*, VII, p. 416 (5th letter to Clarke, 107).

40. *Phil.*, VI, pp. 240–1; *Théodicee*, §§206–7.

41. This tension comes out clearly in the important passage in *Phil.*, IV, p. 462 (Loemker, p. 327). The idea that this tension is resolvable, and indeed resolved, in this "best possible" world is a fundamental act of faith with Leibniz (see PNG, §15).

42. *Phil.*, VI, pp. 377–8.

43. DM, §6. Cf. *ibid.*, §5, and also PNG, 10; *Theodicée*, §208.

44. *Phil.*, III, p. 582 (Loemker, p. 664).

45. *Loc. cit.*

46. Here the use of "uniformement" rules out the asymptotic possibility.

47. 5th letter to Clarke, §74.

48. The themes treated in this section are developed extensively in two brief memoranda: *De progressu in infinitum* (1694/1696?) in Grua (ed.), *Textes inédits*, pp. 94–5; and *An mundus perfectione crescat*, found in *ibid.*, p. 95.

49. "... our happiness will never consist, and ought not to consist, in a full enjoyment, in which there would be nothing further to desire, and which would render our spirit stupid, but rather in a perpetual advance (progrès) to new pleasures and new perfections" (PNG, §18).

50. *Phil.*, VII, pp. 307–8 (Loemker, p. 490).

51. Russell, *Critical Exposition*, p. vi.

NAME INDEX

SUBJECT INDEX

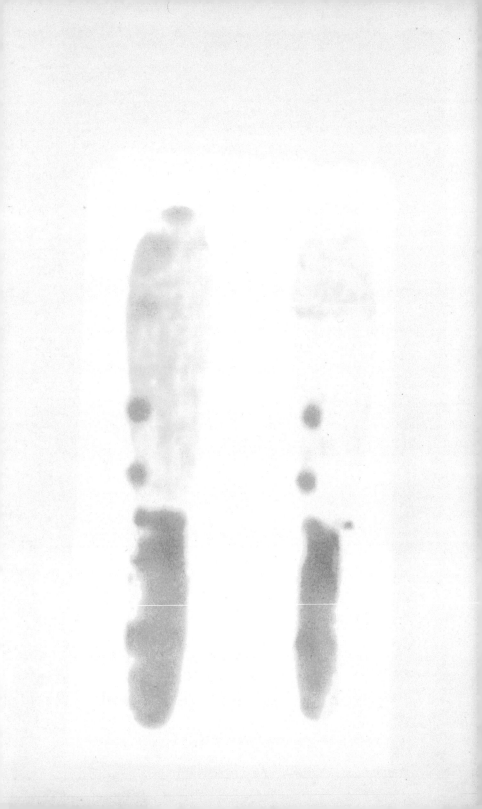

DATE DUE

GAYLORD   PRINTED IN U.S.A.